AF481655

GROW 'N' GLOW

LIFE SKILLS EDUCATION AT SECONDARY STAGE

DR MEENAKSHI NARULA

Copyright © Dr Meenakshi Narula
All Rights Reserved.

This book has been self-published with all reasonable efforts taken to make the material error-free by the author. No part of this book shall be used, reproduced in any manner whatsoever without written permission from the author, except in the case of brief quotations embodied in critical articles and reviews.

The Author of this book is solely responsible and liable for its content including but not limited to the views, representations, descriptions, statements, information, opinions and references ["Content"]. The Content of this book shall not constitute or be construed or deemed to reflect the opinion or expression of the Publisher or Editor. Neither the Publisher nor Editor endorse or approve the Content of this book or guarantee the reliability, accuracy or completeness of the Content published herein and do not make any representations or warranties of any kind, express or implied, including but not limited to the implied warranties of merchantability, fitness for a particular purpose. The Publisher and Editor shall not be liable whatsoever for any errors, omissions, whether such errors or omissions result from negligence, accident, or any other cause or claims for loss or damages of any kind, including without limitation, indirect or consequential loss or damage arising out of use, inability to use, or about the reliability, accuracy or sufficiency of the information contained in this book.

Made with ♥ on the Notion Press Platform
www.notionpress.com

This book is dedicated to all the students who have inspired me with their curiosity, creativity, and resilience. It is my sincere hope that this book will serve as a resource to help you develop the life skills you need to succeed in your personal and professional lives.

I would also like to dedicate this book to my family, whose unwavering support and encouragement have been a source of strength and inspiration throughout my career. Your love and encouragement have been invaluable in helping me pursue my passion for education and life skills development.

Lastly, I would like to dedicate this book to all the educators, researchers, and practitioners who have contributed to the development of life skills education. Your tireless efforts and dedication to improving the lives of students have been a source of inspiration and motivation for me, and I am deeply grateful for all that you do.

Contents

Contents

Social Harmony

National Integration

Differently-abled Individuals

Vulnerable And Marhinalised Groups

Foreword

It is my pleasure to write the foreword for this insightful book on life skills education at the secondary school stage by Dr. Meenakshi Narula. As an expert in education and life skills development, Dr. Narula has provided a valuable resource for educators, parents, and students alike.

In today's rapidly changing world, it is more important than ever to equip our students with the necessary life skills to succeed in all aspects of their lives. This book provides a comprehensive overview of the key life skills that are essential for students at the secondary school stage, including communication, critical thinking, problem-solving, decision-making, and many others.

Dr. Narula's approach to life skills education is both practical and engaging, with numerous examples, case studies, and activities to help teachers and students apply these life skills in real-world situations. Her deep understanding of the challenges faced by students at the secondary school stage, combined with her expertise in education and life skills development, makes this book an invaluable resource for anyone interested in supporting the growth and development of our future leaders.

I highly recommend this book to anyone interested in enhancing their life skills education or supporting the growth and development of young people. It is a must-read for educators, parents, and students who are committed to preparing the next generation of leaders for success in a rapidly changing world.

Lekh Raj

Preface

Dr Meenakshi Narula

It is my pleasure to present this book on life skills education at the secondary school stage. Life skills education is an important component of holistic education and equips students with the necessary skills to lead a successful and fulfilling life. As a lifelong educator and a passionate advocate for the importance of life skills education, I have witnessed firsthand the positive impact it can have on students' lives.

In this book, I aim to provide a comprehensive overview of the key life skills that are essential for students at the secondary school stage. Drawing on my extensive experience as an educator, researcher, and practitioner, I have identified the most important life skills that students need to succeed in today's fast-paced and complex world.

The book is divided into several chapters, each focusing on a specific life skill. I have provided a detailed analysis of each life skill, including its definition, importance, and strategies for teaching and learning. In addition, I have included numerous examples, case studies, and practical activities to help teachers and students understand and apply these life skills in their everyday lives.

My hope is that this book will serve as a valuable resource for educators, parents, and students who are interested in enhancing their life skills education. I believe that by equipping students with the necessary life skills, we can help them lead happier, healthier, and more successful lives.

I would like to express my sincere gratitude to all the educators, researchers, and practitioners who have contributed to the development of life skills education. Their insights and contributions have been invaluable in shaping this book. I would also like to thank my family and colleagues for their unwavering support and encouragement throughout this project.

CHAPTER ONE

Life Skills (Concept)

Life skills are a set of abilities and competencies that enable individuals to effectively navigate the challenges and demands of everyday life. These skills are essential for personal and social development, and they include a range of abilities such as problem-solving, decision-making, critical thinking, communication, empathy, self-awareness, and self-management. Life skills are not specific to any particular domain or situation; they are transferable and applicable across a wide range of contexts. Life skills education aims to equip individuals with the necessary skills and knowledge to manage their lives in a positive and productive way.

Concept of Life Skills at Secondary School Stage

Life skills are the abilities and knowledge that enable individuals to effectively navigate their daily lives, both in personal and professional domains. The secondary school stage, which typically covers students between the ages of 11 and 18, is an ideal time to develop and enhance life skills as students transition from childhood to adulthood.

Some of the essential life skills that can be taught at the secondary school stage are:

Communication: Communication is the foundation of relationships, and students should learn how to communicate effectively with others in different settings. This includes developing verbal, nonverbal, and written communication skills.

Problem-solving: Students should be equipped with critical thinking and problem-solving skills to help them tackle complex issues in real-life situations.

Decision-making: Adolescence is a critical period in which students begin to make independent decisions, and they should learn how to make informed decisions based on their values, preferences, and experiences.

Time management: Managing time effectively is an important life skill that will help students balance their academic and extracurricular activities, and prepare them for the demands of the workforce.

Financial literacy: Students should learn basic financial literacy skills, such as budgeting, saving, and investing, to help them make sound financial decisions in the future.

Self-awareness: Secondary school students should develop self-awareness skills to help them identify their strengths and weaknesses, manage their emotions, and build self-confidence.

Teamwork: Working in teams is essential in almost all aspects of life, and students should learn how to collaborate with others, communicate effectively, and solve problems together.

Teaching life skills in secondary school can provide students with a solid foundation for success in various aspects of their lives. It can help them build strong relationships, make sound decisions, manage their time and finances, and navigate their professional and personal lives effectively.

CHAPTER TWO

Life Skills (Scope)

The scope of life skills at the secondary school stage is vast and includes a broad range of skills that are essential for students' personal and professional development. Here are some examples of the scope of life skills at the secondary school stage:

Personal Development: Secondary school students should be equipped with life skills that help them develop a positive self-image, manage their emotions, and develop healthy relationships.

Academic Development: Life skills that can help students succeed academically include critical thinking, problem-solving, time management, and effective communication.

Career Development: Students should develop life skills that are relevant to their future careers, such as teamwork, leadership, and decision-making.

Financial Literacy: Secondary school students should learn basic financial literacy skills that will enable them to manage their finances effectively and make informed decisions about money.

Health and Well-being: Life skills related to health and well-being can include stress management, coping strategies, and self-care.

Social Responsibility: Students should learn about their responsibilities as members of a community, such as volunteering, environmental awareness, and social justice issues.

The scope of life skills at the secondary school stage is significant, and teaching these skills can have a profound impact on students' lives. By developing life skills, students can build self-confidence, achieve academic success, and prepare for their future careers. Additionally, life skills can help students navigate the challenges they may face in their personal and professional lives and lead fulfilling and meaningful lives.

CHAPTER THREE

Life Skills (Importance)

Teaching life skills at the secondary school stage is essential for several reasons. Here are some of the reasons why teaching life skills are important at the secondary school stage:

Helps with Personal Development: The secondary school stage is a crucial period of personal development, and teaching life skills can help students develop a positive self-image, manage their emotions, and build healthy relationships.

Prepares Students for the Workforce: Life skills such as communication, teamwork, and problem-solving are essential for success in the workforce. Teaching these skills at the secondary school stage can prepare students for their future careers.

Helps with Academic Success: Life skills such as time management, critical thinking, and effective communication can help students succeed academically.

Improves Financial Literacy: Teaching financial literacy skills at the secondary school stage can help students make informed decisions about money and prepare for financial independence.

Promotes Social Responsibility: Teaching life skills related to social responsibility, such as environmental awareness and volunteering, can help students become responsible members of their communities.

Builds Resilience: Life skills such as stress-management, coping strategies, and self-care can help students build resilience and manage the challenges they may face in their personal and professional lives.

Teaching life skills at the secondary school stage is crucial for students' personal and professional development. It equips students with the skills and knowledge they need to succeed academically, professionally, and personally, and prepares them for the challenges they may face in their future lives.

CHAPTER FOUR

10 Core Skills by WHO

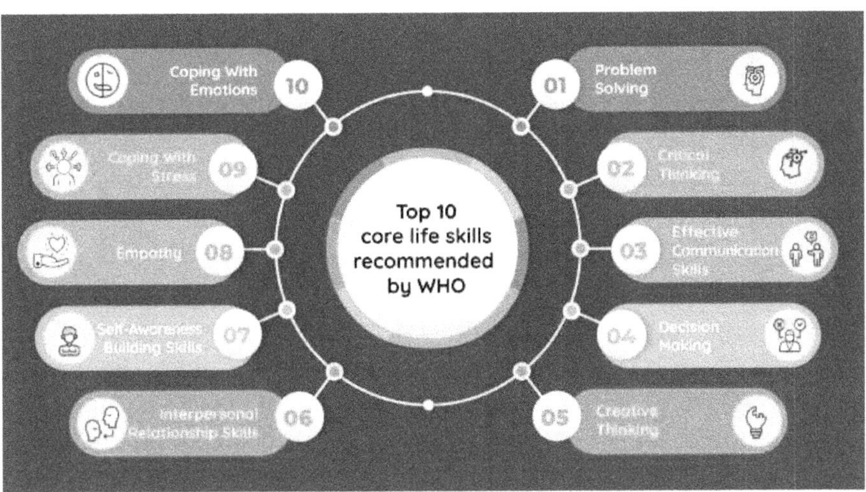

10 Core Skills by WHO

The World Health Organization (WHO) has identified ten core skills that are essential for health promotion and disease prevention. These skills are important for individuals, families, and communities to achieve optimal health and well-being. Here's a detailed explanation of the ten core skills by WHO:

1. Self-awareness: Self-awareness is the ability to recognize and understand one's emotions, values, and attitudes. It involves identifying personal strengths and weaknesses, developing self-confidence, and managing emotions effectively.

2. Empathy: Empathy is the ability to understand and respect the perspectives and feelings of others. It involves active listening, recognizing the diversity of people's experiences and backgrounds, and showing compassion.

3. Critical thinking: Critical thinking is the ability to analyze information, evaluate arguments, and solve problems. It involves questioning assumptions, examining evidence, and making informed decisions.

4. Creative thinking: Creative thinking is the ability to generate new ideas and solutions. It involves imagining new possibilities, taking risks, and using imagination and intuition.

5. Decision-making: Decision-making is the ability to make informed decisions based on available information, values, and preferences. It involves weighing the pros and cons of different options and choosing the best course of action.

6. Problem-solving: Problem-solving is the ability to identify problems, develop solutions, and implement them. It involves critical thinking, creativity, and decision-making skills.

7. Effective communication: Effective communication is the ability to express ideas clearly and concisely, and to listen actively to others. It involves verbal, nonverbal, and written communication.

8. Interpersonal relationships: Interpersonal relationships involve building and maintaining positive relationships with others. It involves empathy, effective communication, and conflict resolution.

9. Self-management: Self-management is the ability to manage one's emotions, thoughts, and behaviors in a positive way. It involves setting goals, developing a sense of purpose, and managing stress effectively.

10. Responsible citizenship: Responsible citizenship involves taking an active role in one's community and working towards the common good. It involves promoting social justice, respecting diversity, and contributing to the well-being of others.

These ten core skills identified by WHO are essential for individuals to promote their own health and well-being, as well as the health and well-being of their families and communities. By developing these skills, individuals can lead fulfilling and meaningful lives and contribute to a healthier and more equitable society.

CHAPTER FIVE

Self Awareness

"The more solitary, the more friendless, the more unsustained I am, the more I will respect myself."

Self-awareness is a critical life skill that involves understanding one's thoughts, feelings, and behaviors. It allows individuals to recognize their strengths and weaknesses, values, beliefs, and personal identity, which is essential for personal growth, decision-making, and building healthy relationships. Here are two examples of self-awareness life skills:

Mindfulness: Mindfulness is the ability to be present at the moment and non-judgmentally observe one's thoughts, emotions, and physical sensations. By practicing mindfulness, individuals can develop a greater awareness of their internal experiences, improve their emotional regulation, and reduce stress and anxiety.

Reflection: Reflection involves taking time to think about one's experiences, actions, and decisions, and examining them critically. By reflecting, individuals can gain insights into their motivations, values, and behaviors, and identify areas for growth and improvement. This skill is useful in many areas of life, including personal relationships, academics, and career development.

Here's a story to teach/ talk about Self Awareness: (*Alex- Fictional Character)**

Once upon a time, there was a young boy named Alex who was always getting into trouble. He didn't understand why he couldn't seem to stay out of trouble, and he often blamed others for his mistakes.

One day, Alex's teacher assigned the class a project to reflect on their strengths and weaknesses. Alex didn't know where to start, but he decided to take the assignment seriously and spent some time thinking about himself.

As he reflected on his behaviors, Alex realized that he often acted impulsively without thinking about the consequences. He also recognized that he had a tendency to blame others instead of taking responsibility for his actions.

Alex's newfound self-awareness allowed him to make changes in his life. He started to think more carefully about his actions and take responsibility for his mistakes. He also began to understand how his behavior affected others and worked to improve his relationships.

Over time, Alex's self-awareness grew, and he became a more responsible and compassionate person. He learned that by understanding himself better, he could make positive changes in his life and relationships.

CHAPTER SIX

Empathy

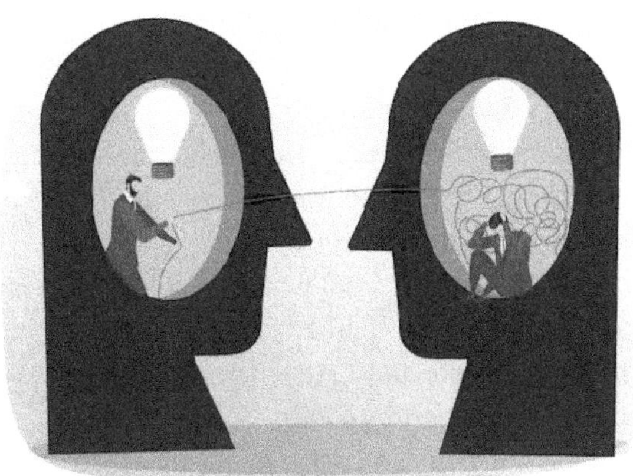

"Empathy is seeing with the eyes of another, listening with the ears of another and feeling with the heart of another." – Alfred Adler

Empathy is the ability to understand and share the feelings of others. It involves putting oneself in another person's shoes and seeing things from their perspective. Here are two examples of empathy:

A friend is going through a difficult time after a breakup. Instead of dismissing their feelings or trying to offer advice, you listen attentively and validate their emotions. You show empathy by acknowledging their pain and providing a supportive presence.

A co-worker is struggling to meet a deadline at work. Instead of criticizing or pressuring them, you offer to help in any way you can. You show empathy by recognizing their stress and offering support, rather than adding to their burden.

In both examples, empathy involves understanding and responding to the emotions and needs of others in a compassionate and supportive way. It requires active listening, open-mindedness, and a willingness to help and support others.

Here's a story to teach/ talk about Empathy: (* Fictional Characters used in the story)**

Once upon a time, there was a high school student named Jane who had always been very self-centered. She tended to focus on her own problems and didn't always consider the feelings of others.

One day, Jane's classmate, Sarah, had a serious family emergency and had to miss several days of school. When she returned, she was visibly upset and distracted. Instead of offering her support or asking how she was doing, Jane ignored her and continued to focus on her own interests.

As the days went on, Jane began to notice that Sarah seemed more and more isolated and unhappy. She realized that she had been so focused on her own life that she hadn't taken the time to consider how Sarah might be feeling or what she might be going through.

Jane began to reflect on how she would feel if she were in Sarah's position. She tried to imagine what it must be like to have a family emergency and to feel like no one cared or understood. As she thought about this, she began to feel a sense of empathy for Sarah.

Jane decided to take action and reach out to Sarah. She sent her a message expressing her concern and offering to listen or help in any way she could. Sarah responded with gratitude and opened up about what she had been going through. Jane listened attentively and offered her support.

Through this experience, Jane learned the importance of empathy and putting oneself in another person's shoes. She realized that by taking the time to understand and support others, she could not only make a difference in their lives but also improve her own relationships and well-being.

CHAPTER SEVEN

Critical Thinking

"It is the mark of an educated mind to be able to entertain a thought without accepting it."—Aristotle.

Critical thinking is the ability to analyze and evaluate information to make reasoned judgments. It involves the application of reasoning, logic, and problem-solving skills to determine the best course of action or decision.

Here are two examples of critical thinking:

A student is given a research project to complete, and they are required to present their findings to the class. The student must gather information from a variety of sources, including books, academic journals, and websites. To demonstrate critical thinking, the student must evaluate the credibility of each source, consider the bias and perspective of each author, and determine which information is relevant and useful for their project. They must then synthesize the information to create a coherent and well-supported argument.

A group of friends is planning a weekend trip and trying to decide which destination to choose. Each friend has their own ideas and preferences, but they must work together to come to a decision that works for everyone. To demonstrate critical thinking, the friends must consider a variety of factors, such as budget, transportation, and activities available at each destination. They must weigh the pros and cons of each option, and consider how their decision will impact the group as a whole. They must also be willing to compromise and find a solution that satisfies everyone's needs.

Here's a story to teach/ talk about Critical Thinking: (* Fictional Characters used in the story)**

Once upon a time, there was a small town that was facing a serious problem. The town's water supply had become contaminated, and the residents were falling sick with waterborne illnesses. The local government was under pressure to find a solution quickly.

One day, a group of senior students from a nearby high school decided to take on the challenge. They formed a team to investigate the problem and come up with a solution. They began by gathering information about the water supply, including the source of the contamination and the types of pollutants present.

As they delved deeper, they realized that the contamination was coming from a nearby factory that was dumping toxic waste into the river. The students knew that they had to act quickly to prevent further harm to the town's residents.

To solve the problem, the students applied critical thinking skills. They considered a range of possible solutions, including contacting the factory owners, lobbying the government, and launching a public awareness campaign. They evaluated each option carefully, weighing the pros and cons and considering the potential risks and benefits.

After much debate and analysis, the students decided to take a multifaceted approach. They contacted the factory owners to demand that they stop dumping waste into the river. They also worked with local government officials to set up a water treatment plant to purify the contaminated water. Finally, they launched a public awareness campaign to educate the town's residents about the dangers of water pollution and the importance of water conservation.

Thanks to the students' critical thinking skills and determination, the town's water supply was eventually restored to a safe and healthy condition. The students learned an important lesson about the power of critical thinking and how it can be used to solve complex problems and make a positive impact on the world.

CHAPTER EIGHT

Creative Thinking

" Everything you can imagine is real." —Pablo Picasso.

Creative thinking is the ability to come up with unique and original ideas, solutions, or products. Here are two examples of creative thinking:

The invention of Post-it notes: In 1968, a chemist named Spencer Silver was working for the 3M company in the United States. Silver had invented a type of adhesive that was not very sticky and did not have many commercial applications. A few years later, another 3M employee named Art Fry was struggling to keep bookmarks in his hymn book during choir practice. Fry remembered Silver's adhesive and decided to use it to create sticky bookmarks that would stay in place without damaging the pages. The result was the invention of Post-it notes, which went on to become one of the most successful office products of all time.

Creative problem-solving in art: An artist wanted to create a sculpture out of old car parts, but struggled to come up with a design that would work. After thinking creatively, the artist came up with the idea of making a giant dragon sculpture using car parts. They used the car parts to create the dragon's scales, claws, and wings. The result was a unique and impressive sculpture that caught the attention of many art enthusiasts.

These examples illustrate how creative thinking can lead to innovative and successful outcomes. By approaching problems and challenges with an open mind and a willingness to think outside of the box, individuals can generate new ideas and solutions that can lead to success in a variety of fields.

Here's a story to teach/ talk about Creative Thinking: (* Fictional Characters used in the story)**

Once upon a time, there was a young artist named Maya who had a passion for creating art that challenged the boundaries of traditional techniques. She always had the desire to create something unique and inspiring, but often found herself struggling to come up with ideas that would truly set her work apart.

One day, Maya was walking through the city when she saw a construction site where workers were using cranes to lift massive steel beams into place. The sight of the beams soaring high into the sky sparked an idea in her mind. She imagined using the beams to create a sculpture that would capture the spirit of the city.

Maya knew that creating a sculpture out of steel beams would be a challenge, but she was determined to make it work. She spent hours sketching out designs and figuring out how to make the sculpture come to life.

Finally, after months of hard work, Maya's vision was complete. The sculpture was a towering masterpiece made entirely of steel beams that twisted and curved to create a sense of movement and energy. The piece was a sensation, and people from all over the city came to see it.

Maya's sculpture inspired many other artists to think creatively and push the boundaries of what was possible in their own work. Her example showed them that anything is possible if they have the courage to take risks, think outside the box, and pursue their passions with determination.

The story of Maya's creative journey serves as an inspiring reminder to senior students that creativity is not limited to one medium or form. By seeking inspiration from the world around them, and daring to think big, they too can create works of art that inspire and captivate the imagination.

Decision Making

"We all make choices, but in the end, our choices make us." — Ken Levine ·

Decision-making is the process of making choices among several options based on a set of criteria. Here are two examples of decision-making:

Choosing a College Major: A senior high school student is trying to decide on a college major. She starts by listing all her interests, strengths, and weaknesses. She then researches the different majors available and considers which ones align with her interests and strengths. She also talks to professionals in the fields she's considering and seeks advice from her guidance counselor. After careful consideration and weighing the pros and cons, she makes a decision on her college major.

Making a Financial Investment: A senior high school student has saved up some money and wants to invest it wisely. She researches various investment options, compares the risks and returns, and consults with a financial advisor. She considers her investment goals, time horizon, and risk tolerance before making a decision on which investment to choose.

Story to teach/ talk about Decision-making (Fictional Characters used)

There was a senior high school student named Emily who was trying to decide whether or not to go on a school trip to Europe. The trip was expensive and would require her to miss several days of school, but it was also a once-in-a-lifetime opportunity. Emily was torn between her desire to go on the trip and her concerns about missing school and the cost.

To help her make a decision, Emily created a pros and cons list. On the pros side, she listed the opportunity to visit new countries, experience new cultures, and make new friends. On the cons side, she listed the cost of the trip, the risk of falling behind in school, and the fact that she would miss several important events at home.

Next, Emily sought advice from her family, friends, and teachers. She asked them what they thought about the trip and if they had any advice for her. Some suggested that she take advantage of the opportunity, while others cautioned her about the risks and costs involved.

After considering all the information and advice she had gathered, Emily made a decision. She decided that the opportunity to travel to Europe and experience new cultures was worth the cost and the risk of missing school. She felt confident in her decision and was excited to embark on this new adventure.

Emily's story demonstrates the importance of decision-making and the process involved in making informed choices. It shows how weighing the pros and cons, seeking advice, and considering personal values and goals can help senior students make better decisions for themselves.

CHAPTER TEN

Problem Solving

"We can not solve our problems with the same level of thinking that created them."

Problem-solving is the ability to identify, analyze and find effective solutions to complex issues or challenges. Here are two examples of problem-solving skills:

Imagine that a group of students is working on a project together, but one member is not contributing equally. The group needs to find a solution to this problem to ensure the success of the project. The problem-solving process might involve:

Identifying the problem: The group identifies that one member is not contributing equally.

Gathering information: The group talks to the member to find out why they are not contributing, and assesses the member's strengths and weaknesses.

Brainstorming solutions: The group comes up with a variety of potential solutions, such as reassigning tasks, talking to the member about their responsibilities, or asking the teacher for help.

Evaluating solutions: The group evaluates each potential solution based on its effectiveness and feasibility.

Implementing the chosen solution: The group agrees on a solution and puts it into action.

Another example of problem-solving might involve a student who is struggling to balance their academic workload with extracurricular activities and other responsibilities. The problem-solving process might involve:

Identifying the problem: The student recognizes that they are feeling overwhelmed and stressed.

Gathering information: The student talks to their teacher, parents, or guidance counselor to get advice and support.

Brainstorming solutions: The student comes up with a variety of potential solutions, such as reorganizing their schedule, prioritizing their tasks, or delegating some responsibilities to others.

Evaluating solutions: The student evaluates each potential solution based on its effectiveness and feasibility.

Implementing the chosen solution: The student agrees on a solution and puts it into action.

Story to teach/ talk about Problem-solving (Fictional Characters used)

Once upon a time, there was a small village surrounded by a dense forest. The villagers depended on the forest for their livelihood, but they faced a recurring problem every year. A group of monkeys would come down from the forest and raid their fields, destroying their crops and causing a lot of damage.

The villagers tried various methods to keep the monkeys away, but nothing seemed to work. One day, a wise old man came to the village and suggested a solution. He asked the villagers to keep some bright and shiny objects near their fields. The monkeys would get distracted by these objects and would stop coming to the fields.

The villagers followed the old man's advice and it worked like magic. The monkeys were indeed fascinated by the shiny objects and stopped raiding the fields.

This story teaches us that sometimes, a simple solution can be found by thinking outside the box. When faced with a problem, it is important to look at it from different angles and consider unconventional solutions.

• 21 •

CHAPTER ELEVEN

Effective Communication

"Communication – the human connection – is the key to personal and career success." — Paul J. Meyer

Effective communication is the ability to convey a message clearly and efficiently to the listener or receiver. Here are two examples of effective communication:

Presentation Skills: During a group presentation in class, a student uses clear and concise language to convey their ideas to the audience. They make eye contact with the audience, use appropriate body language, and use visual aids to support their points. As a result, the audience is able to understand the message clearly and effectively.

Active Listening: During a conversation with a friend who is upset, a student uses active listening skills to communicate effectively. They give their full attention to their friend, listen attentively without interrupting, and ask open-ended questions to better understand the situation. By doing so, they demonstrate empathy and support and help their friend feel heard and understood.

These examples show that effective communication is not just about speaking clearly and articulately, but also involves active listening, empathy, and connecting with the audience.

Here are 10 points to consider for effective communication, along with examples for each:

Clarity: Ensure your message is clear and concise, and avoid using jargon or complex language that your audience may not understand. For example, a teacher may explain a difficult concept to their students in simple terms and avoid using technical language.

Active Listening: Pay attention to the person you are communicating with and respond appropriately. For instance, a counselor may listen actively to their client's concerns and provide support and feedback accordingly.

Empathy: Try to understand the other person's perspective and show empathy towards their feelings. For instance, a friend may console another friend who is going through a difficult time and show them that they care about their well-being.

Non-Verbal Communication: Pay attention to your body language, tone of voice, and facial expressions to ensure they match your message. For example, a job interview candidate may maintain eye contact, sit up straight, and smile to show confidence and professionalism.

Timing: Choose an appropriate time and place to communicate your message. For example, a manager may schedule a team meeting to discuss new project guidelines, rather than informally discussing it in the hallway.

Audience: Adapt your communication style to suit the audience you are addressing. For example, a public speaker may use humor and anecdotes to engage a group of high school students, while using statistics and data to engage a group of academics.

Feedback: Seek and provide feedback to ensure that your message has been received and understood. For example, a teacher may ask their students to repeat the key points of a lesson to ensure they have understood it.

Respect: Treat the other person with respect, even if you disagree with their opinions. For instance, a politician may debate a rival without resorting to personal attacks or insults.

Language: Use appropriate language for the audience and the situation. For example, a nurse may use simple language when explaining a medical procedure to a patient, but use medical terminology when discussing the same procedure with a doctor.

Confidence: Be confident in your communication, but also be willing to listen to feedback and adjust accordingly. For example, a salesperson may confidently pitch their product to a potential customer, but also listen to their concerns and adjust their pitch accordingly.

These points illustrate the various aspects of effective communication, such as clarity, empathy, non-verbal communication, and feedback, and how they can be applied in different situations and contexts to achieve successful communication.

Story to teach/ talk about Effective Communication (Fictional Characters used)

Once upon a time, there was a group of friends who had planned a camping trip. However, when they arrived at the campsite, they found out that they had brought the wrong tent and didn't have any food or water.

One of the friends, John, took charge and suggested that they split into two groups: one group would go to the nearest town to buy supplies while the other group stayed at the campsite to set up the tent and start a fire.

However, one of the other friends, Sarah, didn't like John's idea and thought they should all go together to find a solution. The group was divided, and they began arguing about the best course of action.

John then realized that he needed to communicate his ideas better and understand Sarah's perspective. He asked her to share her thoughts and listened to her suggestions.

Together, they came up with a new plan where they split into two groups but kept in touch using walkie-talkies to make sure everyone was safe and on track.

In the end, they were able to set up their campsite, start a fire, and enjoy their trip, all thanks to effective communication and teamwork. The group learned that by listening to each other's ideas and finding common ground, they could solve problems together.

Interpersonal Relationships

"It is amazing what can be accomplished when nobody cares about who gets the credit." - Robert Yates.

Interpersonal relationships refer to the connection, interaction, and communication between individuals. It involves understanding others, expressing oneself clearly and positively, and building positive relationships. Here are two examples of interpersonal relationships:

Active Listening: Active listening is an important interpersonal skill that involves giving full attention to the speaker and understanding their perspective. For example, when a friend is going through a tough time and wants to share their feelings, active listening involves paying attention, asking questions, and providing supportive responses. It helps to build trust and strengthen the relationship.

Conflict Resolution: Conflicts are common in relationships, and the ability to resolve conflicts effectively is an important interpersonal skill. For example, if there is a disagreement between two friends, conflict resolution involves understanding each other's perspective, finding a common ground, and working towards a mutually beneficial solution. It helps to maintain the relationship and prevent it from being damaged by the conflict.

Story to talk about Interpersonal Relationships with students (Fictional Characters used)

Once upon a time, there was a boy named Tom who had just started high school. He was excited to meet new people and make friends. One day, he saw a girl sitting alone in the cafeteria and decided to go talk to her. They introduced themselves, and he learned that her name was Jane. Tom and Jane started talking and realized they had a lot in common.

Over time, Tom and Jane became good friends. They hung out at school, went to the movies together, and even worked on a group project for one of their classes. However, one day, Tom noticed that Jane was not her usual self. She seemed sad and upset. He asked her what was wrong, and she confided in him that she was having trouble with some personal issues at home.

Tom listened attentively and offered his support. He told her that he was there for her and that she could always talk to him if she needed someone to listen. Over time, Jane began to feel better, and their friendship grew even stronger.

This story highlights the importance of interpersonal relationships and how they can provide support during difficult times. Tom showed empathy and understanding towards Jane's situation, which helped her feel less alone. By being a good listener and offering support, Tom was able to build a strong and meaningful friendship with Jane.

CHAPTER THIRTEEN

Self Management

" Mastering others is strength; mastering oneself is true power" - Lao Tsu.

Self-management refers to the ability to regulate one's emotions, thoughts, and behaviors in a productive and positive way. Here are two examples of self-management:

Time Management: Time management is an essential aspect of self-management. It involves the ability to prioritize tasks, set achievable goals, and manage time effectively to meet deadlines. For example, a student who has an upcoming assignment can manage their time by breaking down the task into smaller parts and allocating specific time slots to work on each part.

Stress Management: Stress management is the ability to manage and cope with stressors in a healthy way. It involves identifying the cause of stress, taking steps to reduce or eliminate it, and implementing coping mechanisms to manage the stress. For example, a student who is stressed about an upcoming exam can manage their stress by taking breaks to relax, practicing deep breathing exercises, and seeking support from friends or a counselor.

Story to inspire senior students for self-management (Fictional Characters used)

Once upon a time, there was a high school student named Sarah. Sarah was a talented artist and musician, but often struggled to balance her schoolwork, extracurricular activities, and personal life. One day, Sarah realized that she needed to learn better self-management skills in order to stay organized and achieve her goals.

Sarah decided to start by creating a schedule for herself that included time for homework, music practice, exercise, and relaxation. She also made a list of her long-term goals, such as getting accepted into an art school or performing in a music competition. Every day, Sarah would review her schedule and goals to ensure she was on track.

At first, Sarah found it challenging to stick to her schedule and stay motivated. But with practice and discipline, she began to see the benefits of her efforts. She was able to finish her homework on time, improve her musical abilities, and even find time to socialize with her friends.

One day, Sarah's art teacher noticed her progress and asked her to create a mural for the school hallway. Sarah was thrilled at the opportunity, but knew it would require even more self-management skills to complete the project on time. She continued to use her schedule and goal-setting techniques, and with hard work and perseverance, she finished the mural ahead of schedule and with great success.

Sarah's experience taught her the value of self-management skills, and how they can help individuals achieve their goals and reach their full potential. She continued to use these skills throughout her life, and became a successful artist and musician.

CHAPTER FOURTEEN

Responsible Citizenship

"Ask not what your country can do for you; ask what you can do for your country."

Responsible citizenship refers to a person's ability to act in a socially responsible manner and contribute positively to society. Here are two examples of responsible citizenship:

Volunteering: Volunteering is a great way to demonstrate responsible citizenship. It involves giving your time and resources to help others without expecting anything in return. For instance, volunteering at a local charity organization or helping out at a community event can help students understand the importance of contributing to their society.

Environmental Responsibility: Environmental responsibility is another important aspect of responsible citizenship. It involves taking care of the environment and making decisions that minimize negative impact on nature. For example, students can take simple steps like recycling, reducing their carbon footprint, and conserving water to demonstrate their commitment to responsible citizenship.

By practicing responsible citizenship, students can contribute positively to their communities and become responsible members of society.

Story to inspire senior students to become responsible citizens (Fictional Characters)

Once upon a time, there was a small town with a big garbage problem. Every day, people would throw their trash on the streets, sidewalks, and in the nearby river. The town's mayor and city council had tried everything to get people to stop littering, from fines to public shaming, but nothing seemed to work.

One day, a group of high school students decided they had had enough. They organized a clean-up day and recruited their friends, families, and even local businesses to help. They made flyers, put up posters, and spread the word on social media.

On the day of the clean-up, hundreds of people showed up, armed with gloves, trash bags, and a determination to make a difference. They worked together to pick up litter from the streets, sidewalks, and riverbanks. As they worked, they talked and laughed and got to know each other. They realized that they all shared a love for their town and a desire to make it a better place.

The clean-up was a huge success. The town looked cleaner than it had in years, and people were talking about the high school students who had organized the event. The students realized that they had the power to make a difference, not just in their town, but in the world.

From that day on, the students continued to organize community events and clean-ups. They started recycling programs, planted trees, and advocated for environmental policies. They inspired others to get involved and make a difference.

Through their actions, the high school students became responsible citizens, showing that even young people can have a big impact on their communities and the world.

CHAPTER FIFTEEN

Negotiation Skills

Chester Karrass: "In business, you don't get what you deserve, you get what you negotiate."

Negotiation skills are the ability to communicate and compromise in order to reach an agreement that satisfies both parties. Negotiation skills are important in both personal and professional settings, as they can be used to resolve conflicts, reach agreements, and achieve goals. Here's a detailed explanation of negotiation skills with examples:

Preparation: Before entering into a negotiation, it's important to prepare by researching the other party's interests, goals, and preferences. This can help you identify areas of common ground and develop a strategy for the negotiation.

Example: Before negotiating a salary raise, an employee may research industry standards and the company's financial performance to better understand their bargaining position.

Active listening: Active listening involves paying attention to the other party's needs, concerns, and preferences. It involves asking questions, clarifying information, and reflecting on what is being said.

Example: In a business negotiation, a salesperson may listen carefully to a client's concerns and needs in order to offer a product or service that meets their needs.

Empathy: Empathy involves understanding and respecting the other party's perspective and feelings. It involves recognizing their interests and needs and showing that you understand and care about their position.

Example: In a divorce settlement negotiation, a lawyer may demonstrate empathy by acknowledging their client's emotional pain and working towards a settlement that is fair and equitable.

Creative problem-solving: Creative problem-solving involves generating new and innovative solutions to a problem. It involves thinking outside the box and considering multiple options.

Example: In a business negotiation, a marketing team may use creative problem-solving to develop a marketing strategy that satisfies the client's goals and budget.

Assertiveness: Assertiveness involves standing up for your own interests and expressing your needs and preferences clearly and confidently. It involves advocating for yourself while also respecting the other party's needs and preferences.

Example: In a salary negotiation, an employee may assertively present evidence of their contributions to the company and their value in order to negotiate a higher salary.

Flexibility: Flexibility involves being open to different options and solutions. It involves being willing to compromise and finding creative ways to meet both parties' needs.

Example: In a real estate negotiation, a buyer may be flexible in their demands and willing to compromise on certain features in order to reach a mutually beneficial agreement with the seller.

By developing negotiation skills, individuals can navigate conflicts and reach agreements that benefit all parties involved. These skills are important in both personal and professional settings, and can lead to more productive and positive relationships.

CHAPTER SIXTEEN

Social Skills

The ability to interact effectively with others, build positive relationships, and navigate social situations.

Social skills refer to the ability to interact effectively with others, build positive relationships, and navigate social situations. These skills are important in both personal and professional settings and can lead to greater success and satisfaction in life. Here's a detailed explanation of social skills with examples:

Active listening: Active listening involves paying attention to the speaker and responding in a way that shows understanding and empathy.

This skill is essential for building positive relationships and resolving conflicts.

Example: In a social setting, active listening can be demonstrated by maintaining eye contact, nodding, and responding with follow-up questions to show interest in what the other person is saying.

Empathy: Empathy is the ability to understand and share the feelings of others. It involves recognizing the emotions of others and responding in a caring and supportive way.

Example: In a work setting, empathy can be demonstrated by acknowledging and validating the feelings of a colleague who is going through a difficult time.

Respect: Respect involves treating others with dignity and recognizing their worth. This skill is essential for building positive relationships and creating a culture of inclusivity and diversity.

Example: In a social setting, respect can be demonstrated by avoiding derogatory or offensive language and treating everyone with equal consideration and kindness.

Communication: Communication involves the ability to express oneself effectively and understand the communication of others. This skill is essential for building positive relationships and navigating social situations.

Example: In a business setting, communication can be demonstrated by presenting ideas clearly and effectively, and actively seeking feedback to ensure understanding.

Conflict resolution: Conflict resolution involves the ability to resolve disagreements in a respectful and constructive way. This skill is essential for building positive relationships and maintaining a harmonious social environment.

Example: In a family setting, conflict resolution can be demonstrated by listening to everyone's perspective, finding common ground, and working together to find a solution that satisfies everyone.

Leadership: Leadership involves the ability to inspire and guide others toward a common goal. This skill is essential for success in a variety of settings, including the workplace and community.

Example: In a volunteer setting, leadership can be demonstrated by organizing and motivating others to achieve a shared goal, such as a charity event or community project.

By developing social skills, individuals can build positive relationships, navigate social situations, and achieve greater success in personal and professional settings. These skills are essential for success in the 21st-century, and can lead to a happier and more fulfilling life.

CHAPTER SEVENTEEN

Thinking Skills

The mental processes involved in analyzing information, generating new ideas, solving problems, and making decisions.

Thinking skills refer to the mental processes involved in analyzing information, generating new ideas, solving problems, and making decisions. These skills are important in both personal and professional settings and can lead to greater success and innovation. Here's a detailed explanation of thinking skills with examples:

Critical thinking: Critical thinking involves analyzing information, identifying assumptions, and evaluating evidence to make reasoned judgments. This skill is essential for problem-solving and decision-making.

Example: In a business setting, critical thinking can be demonstrated by analyzing market trends, identifying customer needs, and making informed decisions about product development and marketing strategy.

Creative thinking: Creative thinking involves generating new ideas, exploring possibilities, and thinking outside the box. This skill is essential for innovation and problem-solving.

Example: In a design setting, creative thinking can be demonstrated by brainstorming new ideas, exploring different materials and techniques, and creating unique and innovative products.

Strategic thinking: Strategic thinking involves considering the big picture, anticipating future trends and challenges, and developing long-term plans and goals. This skill is essential for leadership and business success.

Example: In a business setting, strategic thinking can be demonstrated by developing a long-term vision for the company, identifying key trends and challenges in the market, and developing plans to stay competitive and innovative.

Logical thinking: Logical thinking involves using rational and systematic processes to analyze information and solve problems. This skill is essential for scientific research and problem-solving.

Example: In a scientific setting, logical thinking can be demonstrated by conducting experiments, analyzing data, and drawing conclusions based on evidence and logical reasoning.

Reflective thinking: Reflective thinking involves analyzing past experiences and using them to inform future decision-making. This skill is essential for personal growth and development.

Example: In a personal setting, reflective thinking can be demonstrated by reflecting on past successes and failures, identifying areas for improvement, and setting goals for personal and professional growth.

By developing thinking skills, individuals can become more effective problem-solvers, decision-makers, and innovators. These skills are essential for success in the 21st century, and can lead to a happier and more fulfilling life.

CHAPTER EIGHTEEN

Coping Skills

The behaviors, thoughts, and emotions that individuals use to deal with stress, adversity, and difficult situations.

Coping skills refer to the behaviors, thoughts, and emotions that individuals use to deal with stress, adversity, and difficult situations. Here's a detailed explanation of coping skills with examples:

Problem-solving: This coping skill involves identifying the problem and generating potential solutions. It involves a proactive approach to dealing with stress and can be effective for situations where the problem is within one's control.

Example: A student who is struggling with a difficult assignment may use problem-solving coping skills by breaking the assignment into smaller tasks and creating a study plan.

Emotional regulation: This coping skill involves managing one's emotions in response to a stressful situation. It involves recognizing one's emotional state and using strategies such as deep breathing, meditation, or exercise to regulate emotions.

Example: A person who has received a difficult diagnosis may use emotional regulation coping skills by practicing mindfulness techniques to stay calm and grounded.

Social support: This coping skill involves seeking support from others, such as friends, family, or mental health professionals. It can be effective for situations where the stressor is outside one's control and requires emotional support.

Example: A person who has experienced a traumatic event may use social support coping skills by seeking therapy or talking with a trusted friend.

Cognitive restructuring: This coping skill involves changing negative or irrational thoughts into positive or realistic ones. It involves reframing one's thoughts and beliefs to reduce stress and anxiety.

Example: A person who has a fear of public speaking may use cognitive restructuring coping skills by reminding themselves of past successes and positive feedback.

Distraction: This coping skill involves taking a break from a stressful situation and engaging in a pleasant or enjoyable activity. It can be effective for short-term stress relief.

Example: A person who is feeling overwhelmed with work may use distraction coping skills by taking a walk outside or listening to music.

Overall, coping skills are important for managing stress and promoting mental health. By developing and practicing coping skills, individuals can improve their ability to deal with difficult situations and increase their resilience.

CHAPTER NINETEEN

Life Span Development Theories

Lifespan Development

Life span development theories attempt to explain the ways in which individuals develop and change throughout their lives. These theories propose different factors that shape human development, such as genetics, biology, environment, culture, and social interactions. Here are some of the key lifespan development theories:

Psychodynamic theory: This theory, developed by Sigmund Freud, proposes that individuals pass through stages of development that are influenced by their unconscious desires and drives. According to Freud, personality is shaped by the interaction between the id (instinctual drives), ego (rational thought), and superego (internalized values and morals).

Behavioral theory: This theory, developed by B.F. Skinner and others propose that behavior is shaped by environmental factors, such as reinforcement and punishment. According to this theory, individuals learn behaviors through the consequences of their actions, and these behaviors can be modified through reinforcement or punishment.

Cognitive theory: This theory, developed by Jean Piaget, proposes that individuals pass through stages of cognitive development that are influenced by their biological and environmental factors. According to Piaget, children learn through assimilation (incorporating new information into existing schemas) and accommodation (adapting existing schemas to new information).

Humanistic theory: This theory, developed by Abraham Maslow and Carl Rogers, proposes that individuals have an inherent desire for self-actualization and personal growth. According to this theory, individuals can achieve their full potential through self-awareness, personal responsibility, and positive relationships.

Sociocultural theory: This theory, developed by Lev Vygotsky, proposes that development is shaped by cultural and social interactions. According to this theory, individuals learn through social interactions and cultural practices, and development is influenced by the cultural context in which individuals grow up.

Ecological theory: This theory, developed by Urie Bronfenbrenner, proposes that development is influenced by multiple levels of environmental factors, including the individual, family, community, and society. According to this theory, development is shaped by the interactions between individuals and their environment.

These theories offer different perspectives on human development and can be applied to different contexts, such as education, parenting, and therapy. By understanding these theories, individuals can gain insights into the factors that shape human development and the ways in which they can support positive development across the lifespan.

Jean Piaget's Cognitive Development Theory

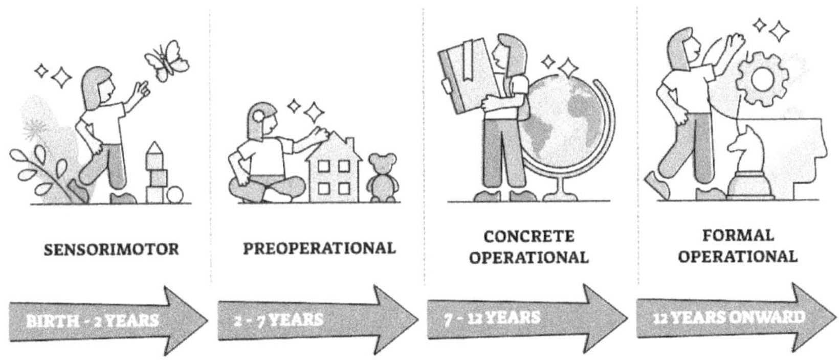

Picture Source and Credit: https://www.wondriumdaily.com/jean-piagets-theory-of-cognitive-development/

Jean Piaget's cognitive development theory is a prominent theory of child development that proposes that children go through four stages of cognitive development, each marked by distinct changes in the way they think and reason about the world. Here's a detailed explanation of Piaget's cognitive development theory with examples:

Sensorimotor stage (birth to 2 years): In this stage, infants develop an understanding of the world through their senses and actions. They learn about cause-and-effect relationships and develop object permanence (the understanding that objects continue to exist even when they are out of sight).

Example: An infant may learn that shaking a rattle produces a sound and develop the ability to search for a toy that has been hidden under a blanket.

Preoperational stage (2 to 7 years): In this stage, children develop the ability to use symbols (such as language and drawings) to represent objects and ideas. They also begin to develop intuitive reasoning and egocentrism (the tendency to view the world from their own perspective).

Example: A child may use pretend play to represent real-life situations and may believe that a tall glass has more liquid than a short glass, even if the amount of liquid is the same.

Concrete operational stage (7 to 12 years): In this stage, children develop the ability to think logically about concrete objects and events. They can perform operations (such as addition and subtraction) and understand conservation (the understanding that physical quantities remain the same even if their appearance changes).

Example: A child may understand that a short, wide glass and a tall, narrow glass contain the same amount of liquid and may be able to solve simple math problems using logical reasoning.

Formal operational stage (12 years and beyond): In this stage, individuals develop the ability to think abstractly and hypothetically. They can engage in deductive reasoning (drawing conclusions from general principles) and can consider multiple perspectives.

Example: A teenager may be able to think critically about complex social issues and develop hypotheses about the causes of global problems.

Overall, Piaget's cognitive development theory emphasizes the importance of experience and interaction in shaping cognitive development. By understanding the different stages of cognitive development, parents, educators, and caregivers can better support children's learning and development across their lifespans.

Mnemonic: (Some People Can't Focus)

S- Sensory Motor

P-Pre-operational

C-Concrete operational

F-Formal Operational

Erik Erikson's Psychosocial Development Theory

Erik Erikson's psychosocial development theory proposes that individuals go through eight stages of development, each marked by a specific conflict or crisis that must be resolved in order to move on to the next stage. Here's a detailed explanation of Erikson's psychosocial development theory with examples:

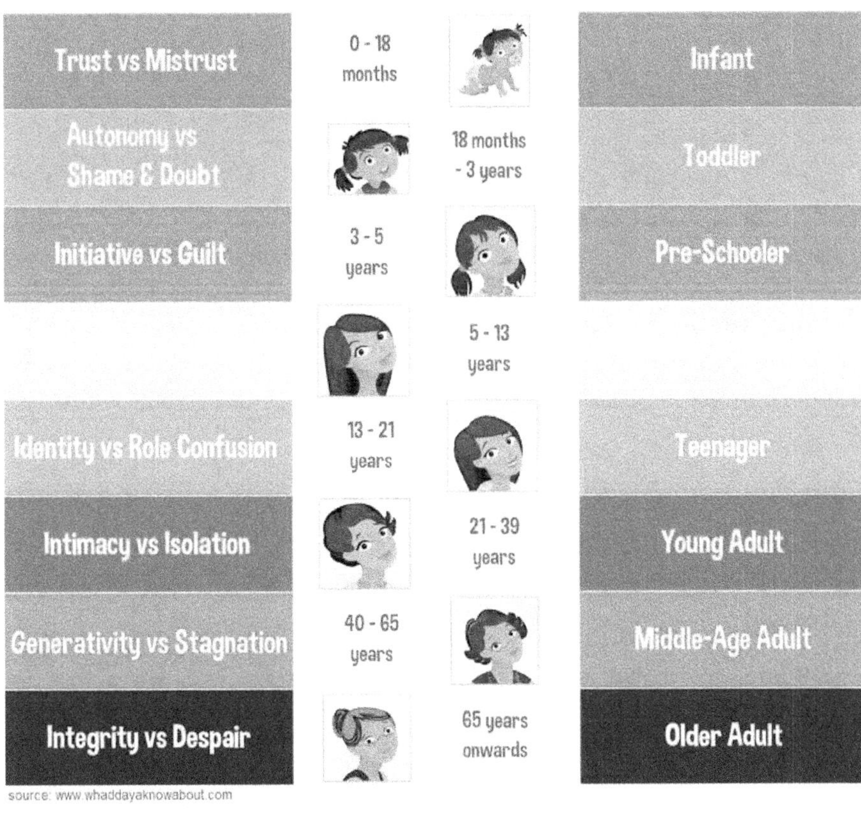

Picture Source and Credit: https://in.pinterest.com/pin/
424675439836713385/

Trust vs. Mistrust (birth to 18 months): In this stage, infants develop a sense of trust or mistrust based on their experiences with caregivers. A consistent and responsive caregiver fosters trust, while neglect or inconsistency can lead to mistrust.

Example: An infant who is consistently comforted and cared for when upset is likely to develop trust, while an infant who is frequently left to cry alone may develop mistrust.

Autonomy vs. Shame and Doubt (18 months to 3 years): In this stage, toddlers develop a sense of autonomy and independence. They learn to do things for themselves but may experience shame and doubt if their efforts are met with criticism or punishment.

Example: A toddler who is encouraged to try new things and praised for their efforts is likely to develop autonomy, while a toddler who is punished or criticized for mistakes may develop shame and doubt.

Initiative vs. Guilt (3 to 6 years): In this stage, preschoolers develop a sense of initiative and creativity. They begin to make plans and carry out tasks but may experience guilt if their actions are perceived as wrong or inappropriate.

Example: A preschooler who is encouraged to explore their environment and take on new challenges is likely to develop initiative, while a preschooler who is constantly told "no" and discouraged from exploring may develop guilt.

Industry vs. Inferiority (6 to 12 years): In this stage, children develop a sense of competence and mastery. They become interested in learning new skills and may experience feelings of inferiority if they perceive themselves as unable to succeed.

Example: A child who is praised for their hard work and accomplishments is likely to develop a sense of industry, while a child who is constantly criticized or compared to others may develop feelings of inferiority.

Identity vs. Role Confusion (12 to 18 years): In this stage, adolescents develop a sense of identity and begin to explore their values and beliefs. They may experience confusion or identity crisis if they are unable to establish a sense of self.

Example: An adolescent who is encouraged to explore their interests and values is likely to develop a strong sense of identity, while an adolescent who is pressured to conform to others' expectations may experience role confusion.

Intimacy vs. Isolation (18 to 40 years): In this stage, young adults develop intimate relationships and establish close connections with others. They may experience feelings of isolation or loneliness if they are unable to form meaningful relationships.

Example: A young adult who is able to form close friendships and intimate relationships is likely to develop a sense of intimacy, while a young adult who struggles to connect with others may experience isolation.

Generativity vs. Stagnation (40 to 65 years): In this stage, middle-aged adults focus on giving back to society and contributing to the next generation. They may experience feelings of stagnation or unfulfillment if they are unable to make meaningful contributions.

Example: A middle-aged adult who volunteers, mentors, or contributes to their community is likely to develop a sense of generativity, while a middle-aged adult who feels unfulfilled in their work or relationships may experience stagnation.

Integrity vs. Despair (65 years and older): In this stage, older adults reflect on their lives and assess their accomplishments and regrets. They may experience feelings of integrity or despair depending on their life experiences and sense of fulfillment.

Example: An older adult who feels satisfied with their lives and experiences

Lev Vygotsky's Socio-cultural Theory of Development

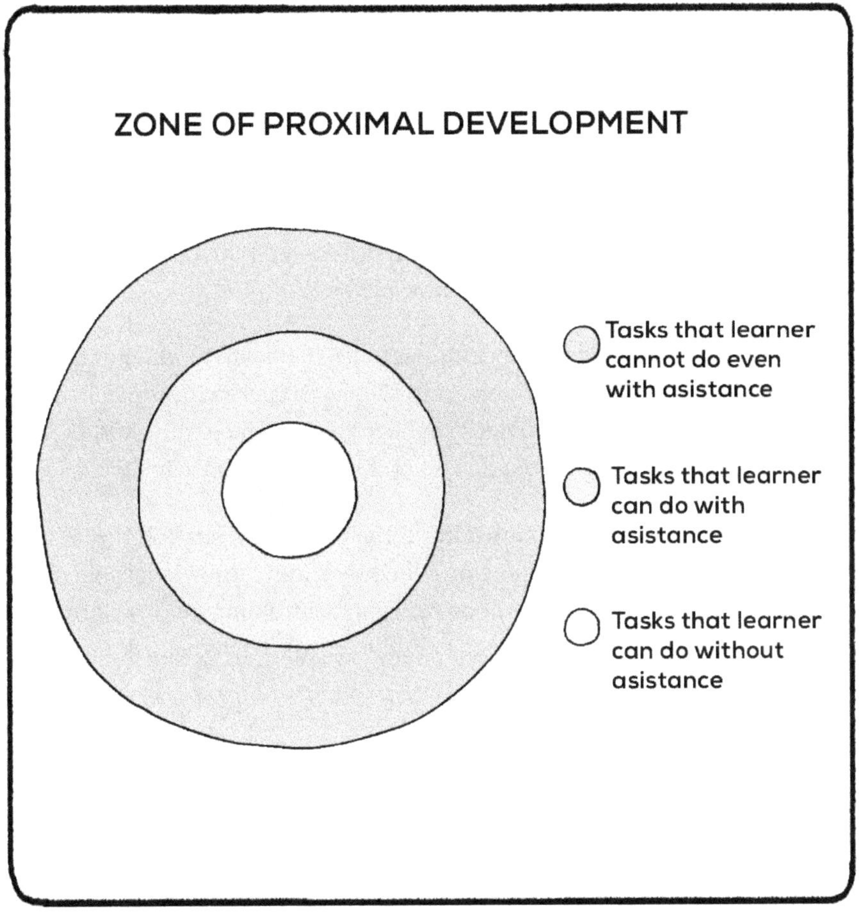

Picture Source and Credit: https://practicalpie.com/sociocultural-theory/

Lev Vygotsky's socio-cultural theory of development posits that social interactions and cultural context play a critical role in shaping a person's cognitive development. According to Vygotsky, children learn through interactions with more knowledgeable others, who provide support and guidance to help the child gradually master new skills and concepts. Here is a detailed explanation of Vygotsky's socio-cultural theory of development with examples:

Zone of Proximal Development: Vygotsky introduced the concept of the Zone of Proximal Development (ZPD), which refers to the gap between what a child can do independently and what they can do with the help of a more knowledgeable other. Vygotsky believed that learning occurs when a child is able to work within their ZPD with the help of an adult or more advanced peer.

Example: A child who is just beginning to learn how to read may struggle to decode unfamiliar words on their own. However, with the help of a more skilled reader who provides support and guidance, the child may be able to read more complex texts that are within their ZPD.

Scaffolding: Vygotsky also introduced the concept of scaffolding, which refers to the temporary support provided by a more knowledgeable other to help a child master a new skill or concept. Scaffolding involves providing just enough support to enable the child to accomplish the task on their own.

Example: A child who is learning how to ride a bike may need an adult to hold onto the bike and provide verbal guidance to help the child maintain balance. As the child gains more confidence and skill, the adult gradually reduces the amount of support until the child is able to ride on their own.

Cultural Tools: Vygotsky believed that cultural tools, such as language and symbols, play a critical role in shaping cognitive development. These tools are acquired through social interactions with others and provide a means for children to communicate and think about the world around them.

Example: A child who is learning a second language may struggle to express themselves or understand others until they become more proficient in the language. As the child becomes more comfortable with the language and acquires new vocabulary, they are able to communicate more effectively with others.

Private Speech: Vygotsky also proposed that private speech, or self-directed speech, plays an important role in cognitive development. Private speech is thought to serve as a tool for self-regulation and problem-solving.

Example: A child who is trying to complete a challenging puzzle may talk to themselves as a way to help them stay focused and work through the problem. As the child becomes more proficient at solving puzzles, they may rely less on private speech as a cognitive tool.

In summary, Vygotsky's socio-cultural theory of development emphasizes the importance of social interactions and cultural context in shaping cognitive development. Through interactions with more knowledgeable others, children are able to gradually acquire new skills and concepts, and cultural tools such as language and symbols play a critical role in this process.

Urie Bronfenbrenner's Ecological Systems Theory

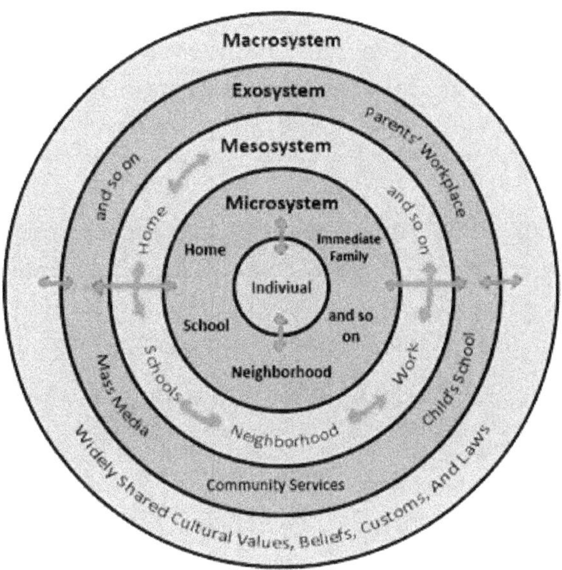

Picture Source and Credit: https://psychology.fandom.com/wiki/ Bioecological_model

Urie Bronfenbrenner's ecological systems theory posits that a person's development is shaped by a complex system of interactions between different environmental factors. These factors can be divided into different levels, ranging from the immediate microsystem to the larger macro system. Here is a detailed explanation of Bronfenbrenner's ecological systems theory with easy examples:

Microsystem: The microsystem refers to the immediate environment that a person interacts with on a daily basis. This includes family, school, peers, and other community groups.

Example: A child's family would be considered part of their microsystem. This includes the child's parents, siblings, and other family members who play an active role in the child's life.

Mesosystem: The mesosystem refers to the relationships and interactions between different parts of the microsystem. This includes the connections between the family and the school or the family and the child's peer group.

Example: A child's mesosystem might include the relationship between their parents and their teacher. This could involve communication between the parents and teacher about the child's progress, or the teacher providing recommendations for activities to support the child's learning at home.

Exosystem: The exosystem refers to environmental factors that indirectly influence a person's development, such as the parent's workplace, media, or government policies.

Example: A child's exosystem might include the impact of the parent's work schedule on the child's daily routine, or the availability of resources in the community, such as parks or after-school programs.

Macrosystem: The macrosystem refers to the larger cultural context in which a person lives. This includes the culture, customs, laws, and values of the broader society.

Example: A child's macro system might include the laws and policies that govern education or healthcare in their country or the cultural values and beliefs of their community or religion.

Chronosystem: The chronosystem refers to the influence of time on a person's development, including the historical and socio-cultural context in which a person lives.

Example: A child's chronosystem might include the impact of technological advancements on their learning opportunities, or the influence of historical events, such as war or economic depression, on their family's access to resources.

In summary, Bronfenbrenner's ecological systems theory emphasizes the complex interactions between different environmental factors in shaping a person's development. By considering the influence of different levels of environmental factors, including the microsystem, mesosystem, exosystem, macrosystem, and chronosystem, this theory provides a comprehensive framework for understanding the complex interactions that influence a person's development.

CHAPTER TWENTY

Pillars of Education and Life Skills

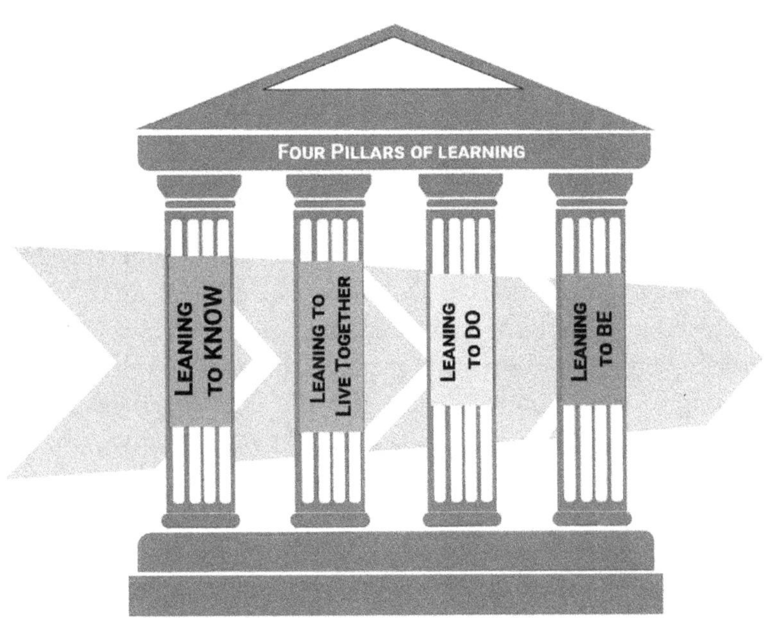

Picture Source and Credit : https://www.peace.school.nz/post/the-four-pillars-of-learning

The Four Pillars of Education is a framework developed by the United Nations Educational, Scientific and Cultural Organization (UNESCO) to identify the essential elements of a complete education. These pillars include learning to know, learning to do, learning to be, and learning to live together. Each pillar highlights a different aspect of education and emphasizes the importance of developing specific life skills. Here is a detailed explanation of the four pillars of education and their corresponding life skills with examples:

Learning to Know: This pillar emphasizes the importance of acquiring knowledge, skills, and competencies through formal and informal learning opportunities.

Life Skills: Critical thinking, problem solving, creativity, and communication skills.

Example: A student who is learning about environmental issues might use critical thinking skills to analyze the causes and effects of pollution, problem-solving skills to identify possible solutions, creativity to generate new ideas for reducing waste, and communication skills to share their findings with others.

Learning to Do: This pillar focuses on the importance of developing practical and vocational skills that enable individuals to apply knowledge in real-world situations.

Life Skills: Adaptability, resilience, initiative, and entrepreneurship.

Example: A student who is interested in starting a business might need to develop adaptability skills to adjust to changing market conditions, resilience to cope with setbacks, the initiative to identify new opportunities, and entrepreneurship skills to manage the business effectively.

Learning to Be: This pillar highlights the importance of developing personal values, attitudes, and beliefs that support positive growth and development.

Life Skills: Self-awareness, self-esteem, self-regulation, and empathy.

Example: A student who is learning about different cultures might develop self-awareness of their own cultural biases, self-esteem to interact with people from different backgrounds, self-regulation to manage their emotions and behavior in multicultural settings, and empathy to understand and appreciate different perspectives.

Learning to Live Together: This pillar emphasizes the importance of developing social and emotional skills that enable individuals to live and work effectively with others in a diverse and globalized world.

Life Skills: Respect, cooperation, teamwork, and conflict resolution.

Example: A student who is participating in a group project might need to demonstrate respect for their peers, cooperate effectively with others, work as a team to achieve common goals, and resolve conflicts in a constructive and respectful manner.

In summary, the Four Pillars of Education provide a comprehensive framework for developing essential life skills across different domains of learning. By emphasizing the importance of learning to know, learning to do, learning to be, and learning to live together, this framework highlights the interconnectedness of different life skills and their relevance to personal and social development.

CHAPTER TWENTY-ONE

Life Skills in Social Context

Life skills are not only essential for individual growth and development, but they also play an important role in shaping and transforming the social context in which individuals live. Here are some ways in which life skills can impact the social context:

Communication skills: Effective communication skills are crucial for building positive relationships and promoting social cohesion. By learning how to communicate clearly, listen actively, and express oneself appropriately, individuals can foster trust, respect, and understanding in their interactions with others.

Empathy: The ability to understand and appreciate different perspectives is a key life skill that can promote social harmony and reduce conflict. By developing empathy, individuals can learn to appreciate diversity, avoid stereotypes, and treat others with kindness and compassion.

Conflict resolution: Conflicts are a natural part of social interaction, but how they are resolved can have a significant impact on the social context. By learning how to manage conflicts constructively, individuals can prevent them from escalating into violence or hostility and build stronger, more resilient relationships.

Teamwork: Collaboration and teamwork are essential for achieving shared goals and promoting collective well-being. By developing teamwork skills, individuals can learn to work effectively with others, respect different roles and contributions, and build a sense of shared responsibility.

Cultural competence: In a diverse and globalized world, cultural competence is an important life skill that can promote social inclusion and reduce discrimination. By learning about different cultures, customs, and traditions, individuals can develop a greater appreciation for diversity and foster cross-cultural understanding.

In summary, life skills are not only important for individual growth and development but also play a critical role in shaping the social context in which individuals live. By promoting positive communication, empathy, conflict resolution, teamwork, and cultural competence, individuals can help to build more inclusive, harmonious, and resilient communities.

Media Influence

Media influence can have a significant impact on the development of life skills, both positively and negatively. Here are some ways in which media can influence life skills:

Communication skills: Media can provide models for effective communication, such as through movies, television shows, and podcasts. However, media can also promote negative communication patterns, such as bullying and aggressive behavior, which can hinder the development of positive communication skills.

Empathy: Media can help to promote empathy by providing opportunities to see and understand the experiences of others, such as through documentaries and news coverage. However, media can also desensitize individuals to the suffering of others by promoting violent or dehumanizing content, which can hinder the development of empathy.

Critical thinking: Media can provide opportunities for critical thinking by presenting complex issues and perspectives, such as through news analysis and investigative journalism. However, media can also promote uncritical acceptance of information and ideas, particularly in the context of social media and other online platforms.

Digital literacy: Media can help to promote digital literacy by providing opportunities for individuals to learn and practice online skills, such as through online tutorials and educational apps. However, media can also promote negative online behaviors, such as cyberbullying and excessive screen time, which can hinder the development of positive digital literacy skills.

Social skills: Media can provide opportunities for social connection and community building, such as through online forums and social media groups. However, media can also promote negative social behaviors, such as trolling and online harassment, which can hinder the development of positive social skills.

In summary, media influence can have both positive and negative impacts on the development of life skills. By promoting positive communication, empathy, critical thinking, digital literacy, and social skills, media can be a powerful tool for promoting individual growth and development. However, it is important to be aware of the potential negative effects of media and to actively seek out positive media content and experiences.

Social Harmony

Social harmony is essential for promoting a peaceful and prosperous society. Here are some life skills that can contribute to social harmony:

Empathy: Empathy is the ability to understand and appreciate different perspectives and experiences. By developing empathy, individuals can learn to appreciate diversity, avoid stereotypes, and treat others with kindness and compassion. Empathy can help to build bridges between different groups and promote a sense of shared humanity.

Conflict resolution: Conflict is a natural part of social interaction, but how it is resolved can have a significant impact on social harmony. By learning how to manage conflicts constructively, individuals can prevent them from escalating into violence or hostility and build stronger, more resilient relationships. Conflict resolution skills can help to promote mutual understanding and respect, and can lead to more peaceful and harmonious communities.

Communication skills: Effective communication is crucial for building positive relationships and promoting social cohesion. By learning how to communicate clearly, listen actively, and express oneself appropriately, individuals can foster trust, respect, and understanding in their interactions with others. Good communication skills can help to prevent misunderstandings and conflicts, and can promote positive social interactions.

Cultural competence: In a diverse and globalized world, cultural competence is an important life skill that can promote social inclusion and reduce discrimination. By learning about different cultures, customs, and traditions, individuals can develop a greater appreciation for diversity and foster cross-cultural understanding. Cultural competence can help to break down barriers between different groups and promote social harmony.

Respect for human rights: Respecting human rights is essential for promoting social harmony. By understanding and valuing the inherent dignity and worth of every individual, individuals can contribute to a society that is based on justice, equality, and respect for all. Respecting human rights can help to prevent discrimination, violence, and oppression, and can promote social harmony based on shared values and principles.

In summary, developing life skills such as empathy, conflict resolution, communication, cultural competence, and respect for human rights can contribute to social harmony by promoting understanding, respect, and positive social interactions. These skills are essential for building strong and resilient communities that are based on mutual respect and shared values.

National Integration

National integration is the process of bringing together people from different regions, ethnicities, religions, and languages to form a cohesive and united nation. Here are some life skills that can contribute to national integration:

Cultural awareness: Understanding and appreciating different cultures is an essential life skill for promoting national integration. By learning about different customs, traditions, and practices, individuals can develop a greater appreciation for diversity and cultivate a sense of cultural sensitivity and respect. This can help to break down barriers between different groups and foster a sense of unity and belonging.

Tolerance and acceptance: Tolerance and acceptance are essential life skills for promoting national integration. By embracing diversity and accepting others regardless of their differences, individuals can promote a sense of unity and belonging in their communities. This can help to reduce discrimination, prejudice, and conflicts based on differences in ethnicity, religion, or language.

Civic engagement: Civic engagement is a life skill that involves participating in the political, economic, and social activities of one's community and country. By actively engaging in civic life, individuals can promote national integration by contributing to the well-being of their communities and country. This can help to build a sense of shared responsibility and a common vision for the future.

Communication skills: Effective communication is crucial for promoting national integration. By learning how to communicate respectfully and effectively with people from different backgrounds, individuals can build positive relationships and promote understanding and empathy. Good communication skills can help to prevent misunderstandings and conflicts and can promote positive social interactions.

Leadership skills: Leadership skills are important for promoting national integration by inspiring and motivating others to work towards a common goal. By developing leadership skills, individuals can help to promote a sense of shared purpose and create a vision for a more cohesive and united society.

In summary, developing life skills such as cultural awareness, tolerance and acceptance, civic engagement, communication skills, and leadership skills can contribute to national integration by promoting understanding, respect, and positive social interactions. These skills are essential for building a strong and united nation that values diversity and promotes the well-being of all its citizens.

Differently-abled Individuals

Life skills for differently-abled individuals are crucial for helping them to lead fulfilling and independent lives. Here are some life skills that can be helpful for differently-abled individuals:

Self-advocacy: Self-advocacy is the ability to speak up for oneself and make decisions that reflect one's own needs and desires. This is an essential life skill for differently-abled individuals as they often face unique challenges and barriers that can impact their ability to live independently. By developing self-advocacy skills, individuals can learn how to communicate their needs effectively and assertively and can work towards achieving their goals.

Problem-solving: Problem-solving is another essential life skill for differently-abled individuals. By learning how to identify problems, evaluate possible solutions, and make informed decisions, individuals can become more self-reliant and independent. This skill can help individuals to overcome challenges and adapt to changing situations.

Communication skills: Communication skills are essential for all individuals, but they are especially important for differently-abled individuals who may face communication barriers. By developing effective communication skills, individuals can learn how to express their thoughts and ideas clearly and confidently. This can help to build positive relationships and promote inclusion.

Adaptability: Adaptability is an essential life skill for differently-abled individuals as they may need to adapt to different environments and situations. By learning how to be flexible and adaptable, individuals can navigate changes and unexpected situations with ease. This can help to reduce stress and anxiety and promote a sense of independence and self-reliance.

Inclusion and diversity: Inclusion and diversity are important life skills for all individuals, but they are especially important for creating an inclusive environment for differently-abled individuals. By embracing diversity and promoting inclusion, individuals can help to create a welcoming and supportive environment for all. This can help to reduce stigma and promote social integration.

In summary, life skills such as self-advocacy, problem-solving, communication skills, adaptability, and inclusion and diversity are essential for creating an inclusive environment for differently-abled individuals. These skills can help individuals to lead fulfilling and independent lives and promote a sense of belonging and inclusion. By promoting the development of these skills, we can create a more inclusive and supportive society for all individuals.

Vulnerable and Marhinalised Groups

Inclusive education aims to provide equal opportunities for all learners, regardless of their backgrounds, abilities, or socio-economic status. To support vulnerable and marginalized groups in inclusive education, it is important to provide them with life skills that can help them navigate the challenges they may face. Some of these life skills include:

Self-awareness and self-esteem: Helping learners to develop a positive self-image and a strong sense of self-worth can empower them to overcome challenges and succeed in school and beyond.

Communication and social skills: These skills can help learners build positive relationships with others, work collaboratively, and express themselves effectively.

Problem-solving and decision-making: Providing learners with opportunities to develop critical thinking and decision-making skills can enable them to navigate challenges and make informed choices.

Emotional regulation and stress management: Supporting learners to manage their emotions and cope with stress can help them to maintain their mental health and well-being, and be more resilient in the face of adversity.

Financial literacy and entrepreneurship: For learners from low-income families or marginalized communities, providing them with financial literacy skills and entrepreneurship opportunities can enable them to break the cycle of poverty and become self-sufficient.

Cultural competency and diversity: Promoting cultural competency and diversity can help learners appreciate and respect differences, and work effectively with people from diverse backgrounds.

Digital literacy and technology skills: In today's digital age, providing learners with technology skills and digital literacy can help them to access information, communicate effectively, and succeed in the workplace.

By providing vulnerable and marginalized learners with these life skills, inclusive education can empower them to overcome barriers and achieve their full potential.

CHAPTER TWENTY-TWO

Life Skills in School Settings at Secondary Level w.r.t. Children Prone to Exclusion and at Risk

Secondary school is a critical time in a student's development, and for children who are prone to the exclusion or at risk, it's essential to equip them with life skills that can help them succeed in school and beyond. Here are some important life skills that could be taught in a school setting at the secondary level:

Self-awareness and self-regulation: Teaching children how to recognize and manage their emotions, thoughts, and behaviors can help them build resilience and improve their mental health. Self-awareness and self-regulation can help students make better decisions and cope with challenging situations.

Communication and interpersonal skills: Effective communication skills can help students build positive relationships with peers and teachers, resolve conflicts constructively, and express themselves confidently.

Decision-making and problem-solving: Teaching students how to analyze problems, evaluate options, and make informed decisions can help them become independent thinkers and problem-solvers.

Study and time management skills: Helping students to organize their time, prioritize tasks, and manage their workload can improve their academic performance and reduce stress.

Financial literacy: Teaching students basic financial skills, such as budgeting, saving, and managing money, can help them make informed decisions about their finances and prepare them for adulthood.

Career and vocational skills: Providing students with career guidance, vocational training, and work experience can help them develop the skills and knowledge they need to succeed in the workforce.

Cultural competence and diversity: Promoting cultural competence and diversity can help students appreciate and respect differences, work effectively with people from diverse backgrounds, and become global citizens.

By equipping students with these life skills, schools can help prevent exclusion and reduce the risk of students becoming at risk. These skills can also help students to build their confidence, resilience, and self-esteem, which are essential for success in school and beyond.

CHAPTER TWENTY-THREE

Life Skills and Career

Life skills are essential for success in any career. Employers look for candidates who possess a range of life skills that demonstrate their ability to work effectively in teams, manage their time and priorities, communicate clearly, and solve problems creatively. Here are some life skills that can be beneficial for career success:

Communication skills: Effective communication is crucial in any career, whether it's communicating with clients, colleagues, or superiors.

For example, a sales representative who can communicate clearly and persuasively is more likely to close deals and build long-term relationships with clients.

Time management and organization: The ability to manage time effectively and prioritize tasks is essential in any job.

For example, a project manager who can manage multiple tasks, meet deadlines, and stay organized is more likely to complete projects successfully.

Problem-solving and critical thinking: In any career, challenges and problems will arise. Being able to identify the problem, analyze it, and find solutions is a valuable skill.

For example, a software developer who can identify and solve coding problems quickly is more likely to be successful in their job.

Leadership and teamwork: The ability to work effectively in a team, collaborate with others, and demonstrate leadership skills is highly valued by employers.

For example, a team leader who can motivate and inspire their team to work towards a common goal is more likely to achieve success.

Adaptability and flexibility: The ability to adapt to changing circumstances and work effectively in dynamic environments is essential in today's fast-paced workplace.

For example, an entrepreneur who can adapt to changes in the market and pivot their business strategy quickly is more likely to succeed.

Emotional intelligence: The ability to manage emotions, understand and empathize with others, and build positive relationships with colleagues and clients is a valuable skill in any career.

For example, a customer service representative who can empathize with customers and build rapport is more likely to provide a positive customer experience.

Digital literacy: As technology continues to play a critical role in the workplace, digital literacy skills such as basic computer skills, data analysis, and social media management are increasingly important.

For example, a marketer who can use social media to promote products and services is more likely to be successful in their job.

By developing these life skills, individuals can enhance their career prospects, increase their job satisfaction, and improve their overall professional development. These skills can help individuals to excel in their current roles, advance in their careers, and adapt to new opportunities as they arise.

CHAPTER TWENTY-FOUR

Life Skills Training Programmes

Life skills training programs are designed to provide individuals with the knowledge, skills, and attitudes needed to effectively navigate the challenges of daily life. These programs aim to empower individuals to make informed decisions, solve problems, communicate effectively, and manage emotions. Here's a detailed note on life skills training programs, including their objectives and examples:

Objectives of Life Skills Training Programs:

Develop critical thinking and problem-solving skills: Life skills training programs aim to develop critical thinking and problem-solving skills among participants. These programs encourage individuals to analyze problems, generate solutions, and evaluate the effectiveness of their solutions.

Enhance communication skills: Effective communication is a crucial life skill, and life skills training programs aim to enhance participants' communication skills. These programs teach individuals how to communicate effectively with others, including active listening, expressing ideas clearly, and providing constructive feedback.

Improve decision-making skills: Life skills training programs help participants develop decision-making skills that are based on careful consideration of facts and options. These programs encourage individuals to weigh the pros and cons of different options, consider potential consequences, and make informed decisions.

Promote teamwork and leadership skills: Life skills training programs emphasize the importance of teamwork and leadership skills. These programs teach individuals how to work effectively in teams, collaborate with others, and demonstrate leadership skills.

Foster emotional intelligence: Emotional intelligence is a critical life skill that is essential for success in all areas of life. Life skills training programs aim to develop emotional intelligence among participants by teaching them how to manage their emotions, understand and empathize with others, and build positive relationships.

Examples of Life Skills Training Programs:

Youth leadership training programs: These programs aim to develop leadership skills among young people. They teach participants how to lead others, work effectively in teams, and solve problems.

Career development programs: Career development programs aim to provide individuals with the skills and knowledge needed to succeed in the workplace. These programs teach participants how to communicate effectively, manage their time, and make informed decisions.

Financial literacy programs: Financial literacy programs aim to teach individuals how to manage their finances effectively. These programs cover topics such as budgeting, saving, investing, and managing debt.

Health education programs: Health education programs aim to promote healthy lifestyles and prevent disease. These programs cover topics such as nutrition, exercise, and mental health.

Conflict resolution programs: Conflict resolution programs aim to teach individuals how to resolve conflicts effectively. These programs teach participants how to communicate effectively, manage emotions, and find solutions that are mutually beneficial.

In conclusion, life skills training programs are essential for empowering individuals to navigate the challenges of daily life. These programs aim to develop critical thinking and problem-solving skills, enhance communication skills, improve decision-making skills, promote teamwork and leadership skills, and foster emotional intelligence. By providing individuals with these skills, life skills training programs can help them to achieve their goals and reach their full potential.

CHAPTER TWENTY-FIVE

Challenges for Achieving Quality Learning Outcomes at the Secondary School Stage

Achieving quality learning outcomes at the secondary school stage can be challenging, especially when it comes to life skills. Some of the challenges that educators and policymakers face in this regard include:

Limited time and resources: As secondary school students have a limited amount of time in school, and teachers have to cover a lot of content in a short period, it can be challenging to integrate life skills education into the curriculum, especially if the resources for such programs are limited.

Lack of trained teachers: Life skills education requires teachers who have specific training and expertise. However, many secondary school teachers may not have received such training, and this can affect the quality of life skills education provided to students.

Cultural and societal barriers: Some life skills education topics may be considered taboo or culturally sensitive in some communities. Educators may face challenges in addressing these topics without offending students or their families.

Limited access to technology: Technology is an essential component of life skills education, and students need access to computers and the internet to learn important digital skills. However, not all schools may have the necessary resources to provide students with access to technology.

Lack of engagement and relevance: Students may not be motivated to learn life skills if they do not see the relevance of these skills to their lives.

It is crucial to engage students in learning activities that are practical and applicable to their daily lives.

Inadequate assessment methods: Traditional assessments may not adequately measure the effectiveness of life skills education. Therefore, educators may need to develop new assessment methods to evaluate the success of life skills programs.

Limited parental involvement: Parents play a critical role in supporting their children's learning, but some may not understand the importance of life skills education. Therefore, educators may need to involve parents in the learning process to ensure that they are supportive and engaged.

Lack of coordination: Different life skills programs may be offered by different departments or organizations, which can lead to a lack of coordination and overlap. It is essential to ensure that all programs are well-coordinated and aligned with the goals of the school and community.

Resistance to change: Some educators, parents, and students may resist changes to the curriculum, including the inclusion of life skills education. It is crucial to communicate the importance of life skills education and the benefits it can bring to students' lives.

Limited funding: Providing high-quality life skills education can be expensive, and schools may not have the necessary funding to support such programs. Therefore, policymakers and stakeholders may need to advocate for increased funding to support life skills education initiatives.

Overall, addressing these challenges requires a multi-faceted approach that involves collaboration between educators, policymakers, and communities. It is essential to prioritize life skills education and provide teachers with the necessary training, resources, and support to deliver high-quality instruction.

CHAPTER TWENTY-SIX

Evaluation of Life Skills Programmes

Evaluating life skills programs conducted for secondary school students is important to determine their effectiveness and impact. Here are some of the ways that these programs can be evaluated:

Surveys and questionnaires: Surveys and questionnaires can be used to gather feedback from students who participated in the program. This feedback can help evaluate the effectiveness of the program, identify strengths and weaknesses, and make improvements for future programs.

Pre and post-assessments: Pre and post-assessments can be used to measure changes in knowledge, skills, and attitudes before and after the program. This approach can provide data to evaluate the program's effectiveness and measure the extent of learning and behavior changes.

Observations: Observations can be used to evaluate how students apply the life skills they learned in the program. This approach can help assess the effectiveness of the program in real-world situations.

Case studies: Case studies can be used to evaluate the effectiveness of life skills programs by examining the program's impact on individual students. This approach can provide a detailed understanding of the program's strengths and limitations.

Focus groups: Focus groups can be used to gather feedback from students, parents, and teachers about the program's effectiveness. This approach can help identify areas for improvement and provide insights into the program's impact on students.

Cost-benefit analysis: Cost-benefit analysis can be used to evaluate the program's economic benefits and determine whether it is a worthwhile investment. This approach can help policymakers make informed decisions about allocating resources for future programs.

Overall, evaluating life skills programs conducted for secondary school students requires a comprehensive approach that considers various factors, including the program's goals, objectives, and methods. This evaluation should be ongoing and informed by feedback from students, teachers, parents, and other stakeholders to ensure that the program is effective and meets the needs of the students.

CHAPTER TWENTY-SEVEN

Analysis of Life Skills Programmes

Analyzing various life skills programs conducted for secondary school students can help identify their strengths and weaknesses and provide insights into their effectiveness. Here are some factors that can be considered when analyzing life skills programs:

Curriculum: The curriculum is an essential aspect of any life skills program. The curriculum should be well-designed and aligned with the program's goals and objectives. It should also be age-appropriate, relevant, and engaging for secondary school students.

Teaching methods: The teaching methods used in the program should be interactive, hands-on, and experiential to ensure that students are actively engaged and learning. The use of technology and multimedia can also enhance the learning experience.

Teacher training: Teachers who conduct life skills programs should be adequately trained and have the necessary skills and expertise to deliver the program effectively. Teacher training can ensure that the program is implemented as intended and that students receive high-quality instruction.

Student engagement: Life skills programs should be designed to engage students actively in the learning process. The program should be relevant and applicable to students' daily lives, and students should have opportunities to apply what they have learned.

Evaluation and feedback: Effective life skills programs should be regularly evaluated and adjusted based on feedback from students, teachers, and other stakeholders. The evaluation should be focused on measuring learning outcomes and the program's impact on students' lives.

Sustainability: Life skills programs should be designed to be sustainable, with clear plans for ongoing funding and support. The program should be integrated into the school's broader curriculum and activities to ensure its continued success.

Overall, analyzing life skills programs for secondary school students requires a comprehensive approach that considers various factors, including curriculum, teaching methods, teacher training, student engagement, evaluation, and sustainability. By analyzing these factors, program planners and educators can identify areas for improvement and develop more effective programs that meet the needs of students.

CHAPTER TWENTY-EIGHT

Highs and Lows of Life Skills Programmes

Here are ten highs and lows of different life skills programs conducted for students:

Highs:

1. Increased student engagement: Life skills programs can increase student engagement and motivation to learn by providing practical, relevant, and hands-on learning experiences.

2. Improved social-emotional learning: Life skills programs can improve students' social-emotional learning by teaching them important skills such as self-awareness, self-regulation, empathy, and communication.

3. Enhanced academic performance: Life skills programs can enhance academic performance by improving students' problem-solving skills, critical thinking, and decision-making abilities.

4. Positive impact on mental health: Life skills programs can have a positive impact on students' mental health by promoting stress management, resilience, and positive thinking.

5. Improved communication skills: Life skills programs can improve students' communication skills by teaching them how to listen actively, express themselves effectively, and communicate clearly.

6. Greater self-confidence: Life skills programs can increase students' self-confidence by providing them with opportunities to learn and practice new skills, receive feedback, and achieve their goals.

7. Career readiness: Life skills programs can prepare students for the workforce by teaching them important skills such as time management, teamwork, and problem-solving.

8. Positive impact on behavior: Life skills programs can have a positive impact on students' behavior by promoting positive attitudes and values

such as respect, responsibility, and citizenship.

9. Improved relationships: Life skills programs can improve students' relationships with others by teaching them how to build and maintain positive relationships, resolve conflicts, and manage interpersonal challenges.

10. Long-term impact: Life skills programs can have a long-term impact on students' lives by equipping them with essential skills and competencies that will serve them well throughout their lives.

Lows:

1. Lack of funding: Life skills programs may face a lack of funding, which can limit their effectiveness and reach.

2. Resistance to change: Some educators and administrators may be resistant to change and may not prioritize life skills programs in their schools.

3. Limited resources: Life skills programs may face limited resources, including classroom space, equipment, and materials.

4. Lack of trained instructors: Life skills programs may require trained instructors who have expertise in the subject matter and the necessary pedagogical skills.

5. Difficulty measuring impact: Measuring the impact of life skills programs can be challenging, and some programs may struggle to demonstrate their effectiveness.

6. Limited time: Schools may have limited time to dedicate to life skills programs, which can limit the depth and breadth of instruction.

7. Narrow focus: Some life skills programs may have a narrow focus, which can limit their ability to address the diverse needs and interests of students.

8. Lack of diversity: Life skills programs may lack diversity in their approach and content, which can limit their relevance and appeal to students from diverse backgrounds.

9. Limited integration: Some life skills programs may not be integrated into the broader school curriculum, which can limit their impact and sustainability.

10. Lack of follow-up support: Students may require ongoing support and guidance to apply the skills they learned in life skills programs, and the lack of follow-up support can limit their long-term impact.

CHAPTER TWENTY-NINE

Health and Wellness Programmes for Life Skills

Evaluation and analysis of various health and wellness programs can provide insights into their effectiveness, strengths, and weaknesses. Here are some factors that can be considered when evaluating and analyzing health and wellness programs:

Program goals and objectives: Health and wellness programs should have clear goals and objectives that align with the needs of the target population.

Curriculum: The program's curriculum should be evidence-based, relevant, and engaging for the target population.

Program delivery: The program delivery should be appropriate for the target population, with consideration given to factors such as age, culture, and literacy levels.

Program length: The program length should be sufficient to achieve the program's goals and objectives.

Program facilitators: The program facilitators should have the necessary expertise, experience, and training to deliver the program effectively.

Participant engagement: Participants should be actively engaged in the program, with opportunities to apply what they have learned.

Program evaluation: The program should be regularly evaluated to measure its impact and identify areas for improvement.

Program sustainability: The program should have plans for ongoing funding and support to ensure its sustainability.

Accessibility: The program should be accessible to all members of the target population, including those with disabilities or who face other barriers to participation.

Long-term impact: The program should have a long-term impact on the health and wellness of the target population.

In addition to these factors, it is essential to consider the specific content and approach of each health and wellness program when evaluating and analyzing them. For example, programs that focus on exercise and nutrition may have different strengths and weaknesses than those that focus on stress management or smoking cessation.

Overall, evaluating and analyzing health and wellness programs requires a comprehensive approach that considers various factors, including program goals and objectives, curriculum, program delivery, participant engagement, program evaluation, sustainability, accessibility, and long-term impact. By analyzing these factors, program planners and evaluators can identify areas for improvement and develop more effective programs that meet the needs of their target population.

CHAPTER THIRTY

Career and Guidance Programmes for Life Skills

Evaluation and analysis of various career development and guidance programs can provide insights into their effectiveness, strengths, and weaknesses. Here are some factors that can be considered when evaluating and analyzing career development and guidance programs:

Program goals and objectives: Career development and guidance programs should have clear goals and objectives that align with the needs of the target population.

Curriculum: The program's curriculum should be evidence-based, relevant, and engaging for the target population.

Program delivery: The program delivery should be appropriate for the target population, with consideration given to factors such as age, culture, and literacy levels.

Program length: The program length should be sufficient to achieve the program's goals and objectives.

Program facilitators: The program facilitators should have the necessary expertise, experience, and training to deliver the program effectively.

Participant engagement: Participants should be actively engaged in the program, with opportunities to apply what they have learned.

Program evaluation: The program should be regularly evaluated to measure its impact and identify areas for improvement.

Program sustainability: The program should have plans for ongoing funding and support to ensure its sustainability.

Accessibility: The program should be accessible to all members of the target population, including those with disabilities or who face other barriers to participation.

Long-term impact: The program should have a long-term impact on the career development and success of the target population.

In addition to these factors, it is essential to consider the specific content and approach of each career development and guidance program when evaluating and analyzing them. For example, programs that focus on entrepreneurship may have different strengths and weaknesses than those that focus on job readiness or career exploration.

Overall, evaluating and analyzing career development and guidance programs requires a comprehensive approach that considers various factors, including program goals and objectives, curriculum, program delivery, participant engagement, program evaluation, sustainability, accessibility, and long-term impact. By analyzing these factors, program planners and evaluators can identify areas for improvement and develop more effective programs that meet the needs of their target population.

CHAPTER THIRTY-ONE

Life Skills and Peer Pressure

Dealing with peer pressure can be challenging, but having certain life skills can help individuals make healthy and informed decisions. Here are some life skills that can be helpful in dealing with peer pressure:

Communication Skills: Being able to communicate clearly and assertively can help individuals express their opinions and make their own decisions. For example, saying "I appreciate your offer, but I don't feel comfortable doing that" can be an effective way to communicate boundaries and preferences.

Critical Thinking: Critical thinking skills enable individuals to analyze situations, weigh different options, and make informed decisions. For example, before making a decision, individuals can consider the potential risks and benefits, as well as their own values and priorities.

Self-Confidence: Having confidence in oneself can help individuals resist negative peer pressure and make choices that align with their own beliefs and values. For example, if a group of peers is pressuring someone to engage in harmful behavior, having the confidence to say "no" can be empowering.

Emotional Regulation: Being able to regulate one's emotions can help individuals manage stress and anxiety that may arise from peer pressure. For example, using deep breathing or other relaxation techniques can help individuals calm down and make more rational decisions.

Problem-Solving: Problem-solving skills can help individuals identify and address challenges related to peer pressure. For example, if someone is feeling pressure to engage in risky behavior, they can brainstorm alternative activities or ways to spend time with friends that align with their values and interests.

Overall, having strong communication skills, critical thinking skills, self-confidence, emotional regulation, and problem-solving skills can help individuals deal with peer pressure in a healthy and positive way. By cultivating these skills, individuals can make informed decisions, express their boundaries and preferences, and build supportive relationships with peers who respect their choices.

CHAPTER THIRTY-TWO

Life Skills and Suicide Prevention

Dealing with suicide prevention requires a combination of personal and interpersonal life skills. Here are some life skills that can be helpful in suicide prevention:

Self-Awareness: Being aware of one's own emotions, thoughts, and behaviors can help individuals identify signs of distress and seek help when needed. For example, recognizing feelings of hopelessness or thoughts of suicide can prompt individuals to seek professional support.

Active Listening: Active listening skills enable individuals to listen attentively to others and offer emotional support. For example, a friend who is struggling with suicidal thoughts may benefit from having someone listen to their concerns and provide non-judgmental support.

Empathy: Empathy is the ability to understand and share the feelings of others. Being empathetic can help individuals connect with others who are struggling and provide emotional support. For example, expressing understanding and compassion towards someone who is experiencing emotional pain can help them feel less alone and more supported.

Problem-Solving: Problem-solving skills can help individuals identify and address the root causes of suicidal thoughts and behaviors. For example, identifying triggers for suicidal thoughts and developing coping strategies can help individuals manage stress and reduce the risk of suicide.

Crisis Management: Crisis management skills enable individuals to respond effectively to suicide risk situations. For example, knowing how to contact emergency services or crisis hotlines, and providing support until help arrives can be critical in preventing suicide.

Advocacy: Advocacy skills enable individuals to raise awareness and promote suicide prevention in their communities. For example, advocating for mental health resources and support services can help reduce the stigma surrounding mental health and encourage people to seek help when needed.

Overall, developing self-awareness, active listening skills, empathy, problem-solving skills, crisis management skills, and advocacy skills can help individuals deal with suicide prevention in a supportive and effective manner. By cultivating these life skills, individuals can help themselves and others seek help when needed, reduce the risk of suicide, and promote mental health and well-being.

CHAPTER THIRTY-THREE

Life Skills and Substance Abuse

Dealing with substance abuse can be challenging, but having certain life skills can help individuals make healthy and informed decisions. Here are some life skills that can be helpful in dealing with substance abuse:

Self-Awareness: Being aware of one's own emotions, thoughts, and behaviors can help individuals identify potential triggers for substance abuse and develop strategies for avoiding or coping with these triggers. For example, recognizing that stress is a trigger for substance use can prompt individuals to develop healthy coping strategies, such as exercise or meditation.

Emotional Regulation: Being able to regulate one's emotions can help individuals manage stress and anxiety that may contribute to substance abuse. For example, using deep breathing or other relaxation techniques can help individuals calm down and make more rational decisions.

Self-Efficacy: Having confidence in one's ability to resist substance abuse can help individuals stay motivated and committed to making healthy choices. For example, believing that one can say "no" to peer pressure to use drugs or alcohol can be empowering and motivating.

Communication Skills: Being able to communicate assertively and effectively can help individuals express their opinions and set boundaries with peers who may pressure them to use substances. For example, saying "I appreciate your offer, but I don't want to use drugs or alcohol" can be an effective way to communicate boundaries and preferences.

Problem-Solving: Problem-solving skills can help individuals identify and address the underlying causes of substance abuse. For example, if someone is using drugs or alcohol to cope with anxiety or depression, developing alternative coping strategies or seeking professional support can help address the root cause of the behavior.

Social Support: Building a supportive network of friends, family, or peers can help individuals stay motivated and committed to making healthy choices. For example, joining a support group or seeking out positive social activities can help individuals avoid negative peer pressure and build supportive relationships.

Overall, having strong self-awareness, emotional regulation, self-efficacy, communication skills, problem-solving skills, and social support can help individuals deal with substance abuse in a healthy and positive way. By cultivating these life skills, individuals can make informed decisions, resist negative peer pressure, and build a fulfilling and healthy lifestyle.

CHAPTER THIRTY-FOUR

Summary Chapter 31-33

Here are 10 life skills that can help students deal with peer pressure, suicide prevention, and substance abuse:

Self-Awareness: Being aware of one's own thoughts, feelings, and behaviors can help students recognize when they are experiencing peer pressure, suicidal thoughts, or substance abuse. For example, recognizing that a particular situation or social group is making them uncomfortable or anxious can prompt students to seek support.

Emotional Regulation: Being able to manage and regulate one's emotions can help students cope with stress and anxiety that may contribute to negative behaviors. For example, using deep breathing or other relaxation techniques can help students calm down and make more rational decisions.

Assertiveness: Being able to express opinions and set boundaries can help students resist negative peer pressure and make healthy decisions. For example, saying "no" to a friend who offers drugs or alcohol can be an effective way to communicate boundaries and preferences.

Active Listening: Being able to listen attentively to others can help students provide emotional support to friends who may be struggling with suicidal thoughts or substance abuse. For example, actively listening to a friend's concerns and offering non-judgmental support can help them feel heard and understood.

Empathy: Being able to understand and share the feelings of others can help students connect with peers who are struggling with peer pressure, suicide prevention, or substance abuse. For example, expressing understanding and compassion towards a friend who is experiencing emotional pain can help them feel less alone and more supported.

Problem-Solving: Being able to identify and address the underlying causes of negative behaviors can help students develop healthy coping strategies. For example, identifying triggers for substance abuse and developing alternative coping strategies can help students manage stress and avoid negative behaviors.

Social Skills: Being able to build positive relationships with peers can help students resist negative peer pressure and seek support when needed. For example, participating in positive social activities or joining a support group can help students build a supportive network.

Decision-Making: Being able to make informed and healthy decisions can help students resist negative peer pressure and avoid negative behaviors. For example, weighing the potential risks and consequences of a decision, such as using drugs or alcohol, can help students make informed choices.

Communication Skills: Being able to communicate effectively with peers, family, and other support systems can help students seek help and support when needed. For example, talking to a parent, teacher, or counselor about suicidal thoughts or substance abuse can help students get the help they need.

Resilience: Being able to bounce back from difficult situations and maintain a positive outlook can help students cope with peer pressure, suicidal thoughts, or substance abuse. For example, using positive self-talk or seeking out positive affirmations can help students maintain a positive mindset and build resilience.

Overall, these life skills can help students deal with peer pressure, suicide prevention, and substance abuse in a healthy and positive way. By cultivating these skills, students can make informed decisions, resist negative peer pressure, and build supportive relationships to promote mental health and well-being.

CHAPTER THIRTY-FIVE

Life Skills and Wellbeing

Implications from Positive Psychology in Childcare at the Secondary Stage

1. **Cultivating a Growth Mindset:** Emphasizing the importance of effort and persistence, rather than innate ability or talent, can help students develop a growth mindset. For example, encouraging students to view mistakes as learning opportunities and praising their effort rather than just their achievements.

2. **Encouraging Gratitude:** Encouraging students to express gratitude for positive experiences and achievements can enhance positive emotions and overall well-being. For example, having students write down three things they are grateful for each day or encouraging them to express gratitude to others.

3. **Promoting Mindfulness:** Teaching mindfulness techniques, such as meditation or breathing exercises, can help students manage stress and increase self-awareness. For example, leading a guided meditation in class or having students practice mindful breathing during a break.

4. **Building Positive Relationships:** Fostering positive relationships with peers and adults can promote feelings of social support and belonging. For example, promoting group activities that encourage teamwork and cooperation or connecting students with a mentor.

5. **Developing Emotional Intelligence:** Providing opportunities for students to develop emotional intelligence skills, such as recognizing and regulating emotions, can improve relationships and overall well-being. For example, teaching students to identify their emotions and use strategies to regulate them, such as taking a break or talking to a trusted friend.

6. **Encouraging Positive Self-Talk:** Encouraging students to use positive self-talk can improve self-esteem and overall well-being. For example, teaching students to reframe negative thoughts into positive ones or having

them write down affirmations and repeat them daily.

7. Encouraging Goal-Setting: Encouraging students to set specific and achievable goals can increase motivation and self-esteem. For example, having students set academic or personal goals and tracking progress towards them.

8. Promoting Resilience: Teaching students resilience-building activities, such as problem-solving or positive self-talk, can help them bounce back from setbacks and difficult situations. For example, having students identify their strengths and use them to overcome challenges.

9. Emphasizing Positive Emotions: Encouraging students to focus on positive emotions, such as joy and gratitude, can improve overall well-being. For example, having students identify positive experiences and reflect on how they made them feel.

10. Teaching Coping Strategies: Teaching students coping strategies, such as relaxation techniques or positive self-talk, can help them manage stress and difficult emotions. For example, having students practice deep breathing or progressive muscle relaxation.

11. Developing Empathy: Teaching students to practice empathy can improve relationships and reduce conflict. For example, having students practice active listening or perspective-taking.

12. Encouraging Optimism: Encouraging students to focus on positive outcomes and visualize success can increase motivation and reduce stress. For example, having students visualize themselves achieving their goals or focusing on positive aspects of a difficult situation.

13. Building Self-Efficacy: Encouraging students to take on challenging tasks and believe in their own abilities can increase motivation and goal attainment. For example, having students take on leadership roles or work on a difficult project.

14. Developing Self-Reflection: Encouraging students to regularly reflect on their thoughts and behaviors can increase self-awareness and help identify areas for improvement. For example, having students keep a journal or participate in reflective discussions.

15. Encouraging Positive Risk-Taking: Encouraging students to take positive risks, such as trying new activities or standing up for their beliefs, can improve self-esteem and overall well-being. For example, having students participate in a debate or try a new hobby.

CHAPTER THIRTY-SIX

Role of Pre-service Teacher Education for teachers to be Professional and Humane

Pre-service teacher education plays a crucial role in equipping school teachers to be both professional and humane in their approach to teaching. By providing aspiring teachers with the knowledge, skills, and attitudes they need to be effective educators, pre-service teacher education programs can help ensure that teachers are prepared to meet the needs of their students and create a positive learning environment.

Here are some ways that pre-service teacher education can contribute to developing professional and humane teachers:

Developing knowledge and skills: Pre-service teacher education programs provide aspiring teachers with the knowledge and skills they need to be effective educators. This includes knowledge of teaching methods, curriculum design, assessment techniques, classroom management, and instructional technology. By mastering these skills, pre-service teachers are better equipped to create engaging and effective learning environments for their students.

Promoting reflective practice: Pre-service teacher education programs encourage aspiring teachers to reflect on their teaching practice and to continuously seek ways to improve their skills. Through reflective practice, teachers can better understand the needs of their students and adapt their teaching methods to better meet those needs.

Fostering empathy and compassion: Pre-service teacher education programs can help teachers develop empathy and compassion for their students. By learning about the diverse backgrounds, experiences, and needs of their students, teachers can create a more inclusive and supportive learning environment.

Encouraging collaboration: Pre-service teacher education programs often emphasize the importance of collaboration among teachers, administrators, parents, and other stakeholders in the educational community. By working collaboratively, teachers can better support each other and create a more cohesive and effective educational experience for their students.

Modeling effective teaching: Pre-service teacher education programs provide aspiring teachers with opportunities to observe and work alongside experienced teachers. By seeing effective teaching in action, aspiring teachers can learn from these examples and develop their own teaching style.

In summary, pre-service teacher education programs play a crucial role in equipping school teachers to be professional and humane educators. By providing aspiring teachers with the knowledge, skills, and attitudes they need to be effective educators, pre-service teacher education programs can help ensure that teachers are prepared to meet the needs of their students and create a positive learning environment.

CHAPTER THIRTY-SEVEN

Role of In-service Teacher Education for teachers to be Professional and Humane

In-service teacher education plays a critical role in equipping school teachers to be professional and humane educators. In-service teacher education refers to the professional development opportunities and training provided to teachers after they have already begun teaching. It is an ongoing process of learning and development that enables teachers to stay up-to-date with the latest teaching techniques and educational best practices.

Here are some ways that in-service teacher education can contribute to developing professional and humane teachers:

Updating knowledge and skills: In-service teacher education provides teachers with the opportunity to update their knowledge and skills in their subject areas and teaching techniques. This includes learning about the latest research in education, innovative teaching methods, and new technologies. By keeping their skills and knowledge current, teachers are better equipped to meet the needs of their students.

Supporting reflective practice: In-service teacher education can help teachers develop reflective practice habits. Through ongoing reflection and evaluation, teachers can better understand the impact of their teaching on their students and make adjustments to improve their teaching practices.

Encouraging empathy and cultural competence: In-service teacher education can help teachers develop empathy and cultural competence, enabling them to better understand and respond to the diverse needs of their students. By learning about the cultural backgrounds, experiences, and needs of their students, teachers can create a more inclusive and supportive learning environment.

Promoting collaboration and community building: In-service teacher education programs often emphasize the importance of collaboration among teachers, administrators, parents, and other stakeholders in the educational community. By working collaboratively, teachers can share their expertise, support each other, and create a more cohesive and effective educational experience for their students.

Modeling effective teaching: In-service teacher education provides teachers with opportunities to observe and learn from experienced teachers, who can serve as role models for effective teaching practices. By seeing effective teaching in action, teachers can learn from these examples and develop their own teaching style.

In summary, in-service teacher education is a critical component in equipping school teachers to be professional and humane educators. It provides teachers with ongoing professional development opportunities that enable them to stay up-to-date with the latest teaching techniques, and supports their ongoing development as reflective and culturally responsive practitioners. Ultimately, in-service teacher education helps teachers provide the best possible learning experience for their students.

End Note

As I conclude this book on life skills education at the secondary school stage, I am reminded of the immense importance of equipping our students with the necessary life skills to succeed in today's rapidly changing world. Life skills education is an essential component of holistic education and is critical for developing well-rounded individuals who are prepared to face the challenges of life.

Through this book, I have endeavored to provide a comprehensive overview of the key life skills that are necessary for students at the secondary school stage. I have shared my insights and experiences as an educator, researcher, and practitioner, and have included numerous examples, case studies, and practical activities to help teachers and students understand and apply these life skills in their daily lives.

My hope is that this book will serve as a valuable resource for educators, parents, and students who are committed to enhancing their life skills education. I believe that by working together, we can create a more supportive and nurturing environment for our students, one that encourages them to develop the necessary life skills to lead happy, healthy, and successful lives.

I would like to express my sincere gratitude to all those who have contributed to the development of this book, including my family, colleagues, and fellow educators. I hope that this book will inspire further research and development in the field of life skills education and serve as a catalyst for positive change in our education systems.

www.ingramcontent.com/pod-product-compliance
Lightning Source LLC
Chambersburg PA
CBHW052052150726
48002CB00002B/858